Professional Issues:
a Guide for
Undergraduate Engineering Students

Martin A. Afromowitz
Professor, Electrical Engineering
University of Washington
Seattle

About the Author

Martin Afromowitz is a professor of electrical engineering at the University of Washington. He began his career there in 1974 after working at the Bell Telephone Laboratories, Murray Hill, NJ from 1969 through 1974. Prof. Afromowitz attended Columbia University and received his BS, MS and PhD degrees in 1965, 1966 and 1969 respectively.

You may contact him at afro@u.washington.edu.

Acknowledgments

The author thanks his colleagues Professor Maya Gupta and Professor Mark Damborg for their close reading of early drafts of this text, and for their several recommendations and comments. Thanks also to David Slater (UW) and Professor Bijan Sepahpour (TCNJ) for their suggestions. The author expresses his thanks to Rebecca Black for her cover design.

"**It is a great profession**. There is the fascination of watching a figment of the imagination emerge through the aid of science to a plan on paper. Then it moves to realization in stone or metal or energy. Then it brings jobs and homes to men. Then it elevates the standards of living and adds to the comforts of life. That is the engineer's high privilege.

The great liability of the engineer compared to men of other professions is that his works are out in the open where all can see them. His acts, step by step, are in hard substance. He cannot bury his mistakes in the grave like the doctors. He cannot argue them into thin air or blame the judge like the lawyers. He cannot, like the architects, cover his failures with trees and vines. He cannot, like the politicians, screen his shortcomings by blaming his opponents and hope the people will forget. The engineer simply cannot deny he did it. If his works do not work, he is damned forever.

On the other hand, unlike the doctor his is not a life among the weak. Unlike the soldier, destruction is not his purpose. Unlike the lawyer, quarrels are not his daily bread. To the engineer falls the job of clothing the bare bones of science with life, comfort, and hope. No doubt as years go by the people forget which engineer did it, even if they ever knew. Or some politician puts his name on it. Or they credit it to some promoter who used other people's money... But the engineer himself looks back at the unending stream of goodness which flows from his successes with satisfactions that few professions may know. And the verdict of his fellow professionals is all the accolade he wants."

Herbert Hoover, 31st US President
Profession: Mining Engineer

Table of Contents

Introduction — Common Questions

Ask a group of undergraduate engineering students what their most pressing career-related questions are, and you'll find a surprising uniformity of responses.

- What's the best way to get a good job upon graduation?
- What's the job market like?
- How do I make myself more appealing to an employer?
- What are the different engineering jobs like?
- Which area of specialization has the best salaries and the greatest stability?
- How important is an MS degree?
- How do I start my own company?
- How do I get into research?
- How do I negotiate my first salary?
- Which of my courses are most important?
- Should I get an MBA?

These are all great questions, and unfortunately, you may have found that they aren't answered in any of your technical courses! You'll find some guidance, things to think about, and data to help you answer these questions in the chapters that follow.

In Chapter 1, *Will you be Ready to Graduate?* you will find information about building your résumé; the importance of a co-op or internship experience; advice for students for which English is a second language; and some insight into making the transition from the life of a student to that of an employee.

Chapter 2, *Your Earnings Potential*, shows you how salaries differ among engineering jobs; how the average engineer's wages increase with experience; how advanced degrees might improve your salary potential; how your career path may be modified by an advanced degree; and the value of continuing education to the professional engineer.

Did I say "professional"? Just what does that mean? Chapter 3, *Societal Expectations of the Engineering Professional*, introduces you to the concept of "the professional." It's a title filled with huge expectations, responsibilities, and rewards. You can't start too early to get used to thinking about professional issues... that is, *ahem*, **Professional Issues**. I know, it's the title of this book, and most people have some idea of what it means. But many of the most important characteristics of being "a professional" are not known to students who are working their butts off trying to become one. Hopefully, after thinking about the material in Chapter 3, you'll have a clue.

Chapter 4 deals with *The Corporate Enterprise*. I venture to say that most of you will work for an employer (or become one yourself) sometime during your career. Although not every employer is a "corporation" in the legal sense, all employers likely to hire you as an engineer will fall into one of the following categories: a private company; a start-up; a (usually) large public corporation, or the government. Each of these enterprises has a boss, a structure, a chain of command, higher-ups and lower-downs, and it's very important for you to understand where you will fit into your organization. The company structure might influence your potential for promotion, how you will be evaluated for a raise, and perhaps how rigidly your work routine will be controlled. Oh, and by the way, besides doing a good job, do you owe your employer anything else? Like loyalty? An interesting question...

Say you had a terrific interview, and the company is calling you back to discuss a job offer. There is a lot to think about here — is the salary competitive? Fringe benefits? Moving expenses? And what is all that legal gobbledygook they want you to read and sign? See Chapter 5, *The Employment Contract*.

The employment contract raises the issue of intellectual property and patents. Just how does a patent work? How do you, or your company, make money on a patent? Chapter 6: *Patents*.

I left the tough one for last... The push and pull of politics; the exigencies of economics; the science and sentiments of social theory; they all converge on *Outsourcing and the Global Marketplace*, the subjects of Chapter 7.

Guide to the Instructor

This small volume is meant to provide a basis for a ten week seminar course on professional issues of interest to undergraduate engineering students. I have deliberately kept the text brief so that students would be more likely to read it. The topics raised are not fully explored, leaving an opportunity for further discussion and discovery in class, under your guidance. Outside readings and research topics are suggested in the Essay Questions at the end of each chapter.

A course based on this book can easily be used to assess students on several *program outcomes* required by ABET for accreditation purposes. The material is appropriate for students in most engineering programs, but bioengineers may require a separate concentrated discussion of bioethics, which is not presented herein. The outcomes that are addressed include:

- *An understanding of professional and ethical responsibilities*
- *An ability to communicate effectively*
- *The broad education necessary to understand the impact of engineering solutions in a global, economic, environmental and societal context*
- *A recognition of the need for, and an ability to engage in life-long learning*
- *Knowledge of contemporary issues*

Professional and ethical responsibilities are addressed directly in Chapters 3, 4 and 6. Effective communication may be assessed through observation of class discussion, but more significantly by assigning and grading short essays each week. A student's understanding of the impact of engineering solutions may be assessed through discussion or essays addressing outsourcing, as well as some of the unfortunate engineering/management failures in recent times, such as the Ford Pinto gas tank problem and the Challenger disaster, among others. The need for life-long learning is discussed primarily in Chapter 2 in an analysis of technology depreciation rates. Finally, the contemporary issues of outsourcing and immigration policy always lead to interesting discussion, especially when a class comprises native and immigrant students!

A useful stimulant to class discussion is to have students' essays available on-line so that all may read them prior to class. Have fun!

Chapter One

Will You Be Ready to Graduate?

Put your future in good hands ~ your own. ~Author Unknown

Part One: Building Your Résumé

Work Experience

Of course, the first thing a recruiter will want to know is, "How are your grades?" But that is not the only thing a company is interested in. Just as it was when you applied to college, the recruiter will be interested in many things that don't show up on your transcript. Your *résumé*, (from the French for *sum up*), sometimes called a *curriculum vitae*, or CV (Latin for *course of life*) needs to show who you are, and what you are potentially capable of, beyond your grades.

Extra curricular activities, clubs, sports, evidence of leadership abilities, are all important things to mention. But I want to focus on what you can do to build your future employer's confidence in you *as an engineering employee*. And while you're doing that, you'll be building your own confidence in yourself.

One of the most useful things you can do during your undergraduate years is to take part in a co-op or internship program through your school. Most engineering colleges offer such opportunities. Find out about that. You may be eager to get out of school as fast as you possibly can, but take a moment to think about the tremendous benefits that can accrue to you while working for a real company in a novice engineering capacity.

First of all, you will get paid. You will probably get academic credit. You will have a chance to observe how real engineers work. You will be given a job to do that is within your capabilities, even if you are just starting out in your engineering program. You will work with engineers, or for a supervisor, who can serve as references for you in the future. If you're lucky, you might learn which area of specialization in your discipline might be most interesting to you. You might even learn that what you thought you'd want to do *isn't* a good match for you! That's a valuable lesson as well. You don't want to take a bunch of courses learning about something that you'd hate to do later on. You'll learn something about the work environment in your company — it may be very different in another company of a significantly different size, but no matter... every little bit of experience helps. You will learn to rely on yourself. You will figure out how to find out what you need to know to get your job done. You will learn to be creative. You will learn to be successful.

A recruiter reading your CV will understand all these good things. Successful co-op experiences, bolstered by positive letters of reference from your supervisor or co-workers, can be more important than your grades! An employer doesn't make a profit by pinning your glowing transcript up on the company bulletin board. An employer makes a profit by hiring engineers who can get a job done, creatively, efficiently, on time and on budget. If your résumé says that you can do that, you have a big advantage over the A student with no co-op experience.

If a paid co-op opportunity is not available to you, the next best idea is to seek a novice engineering position at a company for which you are paid a small amount, or not at all. It's more or less a volunteer position. OK, no salary; maybe no college credit. But all the other potential benefits that I described above are possible. The key is getting your foot in the door and working with, for, and as an engineer.

In both these situation, you will create a story with your employer. Companies don't like to hire someone into a high-paying job that they don't know much about. With your co-op or internship experience, the company that you worked for is much more likely to be interested in you when you finally get your degree. Of course, you have to have done well. Your co-op or internship story has to have a good ending.

The next best bet is to find part-time jobs while you're in school. Spending the summer soaking up the rays will not help much. Working, even at a non-engineering job, even as a volunteer, will be useful to you. The value is that it shows a prospective employer that you are a motivated, hard-working person; that you believe in contributing your skills to the success of an enterprise. Those letters of recommendation are still valuable, even if they are coming from the manager of a supermarket.

<u>Making Your Knowledge of the World Work for You</u>

It used to be rare to find an engineering student who was foreign-born. Look around your classes now: identifying all the native-born students (and faculty) amongst the huge ethnic diversity at our engineering schools now can be really hard. Engineering has always been attractive to the capable and motivated immigrant. It affords a chance for a stable, good salary, and high social esteem (more on all that later). An immigrant student for whom English is a second language has major hurdles to climb. English language proficiency is very important, and will be discussed later in this chapter. But it would be a big mistake to downplay your cultural diversity on your résumé. Here's why:

Every large engineering company in the United States has an interest in selling, buying, producing, investing, collaborating — overseas. The most obvious countries in this group are China, Japan, Korea, Taiwan, other nations in Asia, the European community (principally England, Germany and France), India, Russia, and many of the countries in the mid-east. Also of great interest are Mexico, and the countries of South America (Brazil in particular). If you have a strong cultural attachment to a foreign nation, if you can speak a language other than English, if you understand the social, historical and political complexities of another nation, you are potentially a tremendous asset to a company that may have economic interests there!

Americans, even highly educated Americans, are generally culturally naïve. We live in a large, powerful country, isolated from most of the rest of the world (save for Canada and Mexico) by two large oceans, and because of our political and economic strengths, our language and culture have spread way beyond our borders. When we travel, we *expect* people in distant lands to speak English to us. We are at a loss if they don't. English is often claimed to be the universal language. After all, it is an official language in about 70 countries, and English speakers account for about 40% of the world's economic activity. It's easy to get complacent, and lose sight of the fact that more than twice as many people speak Mandarin than English, and that China's economy is gaining on that of the US, up to more than 60% of our GNP in 2010. When US companies seek to do business with the rest of the world, they need all the help they can get. Consider this — many business leaders in India or China today may have been students in our top universities 10 to 15 years ago. Consequently, they know the US and how it works from their own experiences. How many US industry leaders do you think might have gotten an MBA in India or China? One way for US companies to overcome their lack of comfort with foreign countries would be to rely on employees that *know* the business, *know* the language, and *know* the culture. These employees can be prime assets to a company, and large multinational corporations need correspondingly large numbers of such employees. This opens up huge opportunities for non-native engineering students. Use it to your advantage! Don't hide what may be your most distinguishing and valuable selling point.

Part Two: Improve your Communications Skills — NOW

Every engineering job in industry will require that you communicate fluently, coherently, accurately and grammatically, both in person, verbally, and through writing. You will be giving oral presentations to your managers, to clients, to colleagues. You will be writing progress reports, technical memos and product descriptions. Clarity of presentation is paramount for an engineer. This is a very important part of your job.

If you feel that your writing skills are not as good as they could be, do not be discouraged. Like any other skill, writing improves with practice. You can overcome any deficiency through concentrated effort.

Many years ago, a reasonably good student in my class used to hand in homework assignments with the most atrocious spelling. This fellow was born in the US, his parents were born here, he had graduated from a fine suburban high school, he had good grades, he grew up in an upper middle class neighborhood, and he would spell the same word three different ways in the same paragraph! I called him into my office to chat one day, and I asked him why he seemed to be such a poor speller. His answer was, "Well, you knew what I meant, didn't you? What's the difference?" I told him that once he got out of school and started working, his co-workers would think that he was uneducated, ignorant and illiterate, even if he had a BS degree. His colleagues would expect him to spell perfectly and use correct grammar, especially since he was a native speaker. He'd get no slack! I told him to use spell-check, and pay attention to his grammar. Well, he graduated, got an advanced degree and even started his own small company. A few years later, he came back to the university to visit. When he stopped into my office, he told me that I had given him the

4

best advice he ever got. He found that indeed, he got little respect from his colleagues until his English language skills improved. It was critically important to his advancement.

Times haven't changed. You will be expected to write *very* well, and make *very* few grammatical or spelling errors. Fortunately, word processing programs will flag many ungrammatical constructions for you, and highlight or autocorrect some of your spelling mistakes. Take advantage of those tools, and strive to improve your English skills. There is no alternative if you want to be known as a serious and capable engineer.

Advice for the Non-Native Speaker

Students for whom English is a second language, and are still struggling with its idiosyncrasies, have an enhanced burden. As you enter the work force, your status as a non-native speaker may temporarily reduce the expectations of your supervisors for perfect spelling and grammar, but you will still need to be able to communicate your message accurately and concisely. There is no getting around the fact that your communications skills will need to improve. Work hard *now* to improve your vocabulary, usage, grammar, spelling, verbal fluency and pronunciation. Take advantage of ESL classes, read English literature and the daily newspapers; write as much as you can, and have a language tutor work with you to correct your compositions. Expand your circle of close social interaction to include native English speakers and consciously work to mimic their speech patterns; take English and technical communications courses. For pronunciation improvement, practice using accent reduction CDs. Your success in attaining excellent communications skills can set you apart, or hold you back. It is an essential component of your professional education.

Part Three: The Transition from Student to Employee

The leap from the life of the student to the very different world of the salaried employee is often the most worrisome concern of undergraduates. If you are the type of individual who had butterflies in your stomach every first day of school for the past 16 years, don't be surprised if they will be fluttering on your first day at work! Here are some things to think about that may allay your fears.

Companies hire new employees all the time, and they are well aware of the insecurities that might accompany a fresh graduate beginning a first job. Your new colleagues will very likely be very supportive and treat you well; after all, they all had similar experiences, and know how you feel. You will often be asked to work with an experienced employee, perhaps for months, to help you learn what you need to know to do your job well. You might be given a tall stack of documents to read, things like company policy and operations manuals, information about medical insurance benefits, vacations, how the company is organized, who does what, etc. Look for what will be expected of you. If that's not immediately clear, ask your mentor.

Large companies often have formal orientation programs for new employees run by the company's Human Resources department. Your company is just as eager to make a good first impression on *you* as you are on *them*! Your employee orientation should:

- ❖ Make you feel welcome and valued as a key player on the team.
- ❖ Explain the mission of the company and the job so you can see the big picture.
- ❖ Give assurances that you will be carefully and patiently trained — not thrown in to 'sink or swim.'
- ❖ Familiarize you with rules, policies and procedures.
- ❖ Help you adapt to your new surroundings, as well as learn who all the players are and how they work together.
- ❖ Establish friendly relationships among co-workers and managers.
- ❖ Ensure that you have all the information and tools you need to do your job.
- ❖ Motivate you to succeed as an integral part of the team.
- ❖ Tell you what's in it for you — in sum, reinforce your decision to join the company.

You may also be surprised at how much new information and technical skills you will need to learn. You may wonder why you weren't taught all this stuff in school. The fact is that the technologies that you are learning in your courses today are likely to be out of date before you even start your first job. The principal reason is that textbooks, written a few years ago perhaps, can't foretell the future.

6

Even senior-level capstone classes are likely to be years behind industrial practice — after all, most companies don't publicly disclose their best tricks in order to keep their competition in the dark. If your professor is doing research in that field, you may be getting more up-to-date information, but maybe not. Where does that leave you, the novice engineer? Back in the last decade, perhaps. But don't worry — you know all the basics. Although you may have never seen this on a course syllabus, what you are really learning in your courses is how to learn on your own! You will be able to learn the new material. Your company will give you time to come up to speed.

The most important thing your company will be looking for during your first few days and weeks is your enthusiasm. You will be well-served by demonstrating your eagerness to learn, arriving at work and at meetings *on time*, dressing appropriately (make note of what your co-workers wear), and showing that you can work with a team of diverse individuals. These characteristics will form the first impressions your supervisors have of you, and your first priority is to make them all positive indicators of your future with the company.

Essay Questions

1) Imagine that you are 6 months from finishing your degree. Search for a job on-line that looks interesting to you and for which you would be qualified. Look at no more than ten sites. Write an essay about your impressions of the job market, and what the available job descriptions tell you about how to improve your chances.

2) Critique your communications skills in a realistic way. What particular difficulties do you have? What would improve your skills?

3) Create a résumé for yourself. Look on-line for some examples. Where are the weak spots? What would you like to do to improve how you look on paper?

Chapter Two
Your Earnings Potential

I have enough money to last me the rest of my life, unless I buy something. – Jackie Mason

Part One: Salary Ranges and Historical Trends

Starting Salaries for the BS Engineer

Engineers as a group have the highest average starting salaries of Bachelor of Science or Bachelor of Arts graduates in any field. That should make you feel pretty good! Starting salaries for engineers vary from year to year and depend primarily on the state of the national and local economy, and supply and demand. Starting salaries of engineers in different fields vary quite widely. A few general trends have emerged over time. The following table of average starting salaries for engineers holding BS degrees in different disciplines was developed through a July 2009 survey by the National Association of Colleges and Employers and summarized in the Occupational Outlook Handbook of the Bureau of Labor Statistics[1]:

Petroleum	$83,121
Chemical	$64,902
Mining and Mineral	$64,404
Computer	$61,738
Nuclear	$61,610
Electrical/electronics and communications	$60,125
Mechanical	$58,766
Industrial/manufacturing	$58,358
Materials	$57,349
Aerospace/aeronautical/astronautical	$56,311
Agricultural	$54,352
Bioengineering and biomedical	$54,158
Civil	$52,048

---

[1] http://bls.gov/oco/ocos027.htm

A consistent feature of these surveys over the years has been the relatively higher starting salaries of petroleum engineers. The data is less useful than you may think, since starting salaries offered by companies located in large urban centers tend to be higher than those of companies situated in smaller cities or suburbs; salaries are higher if the local cost of living, especially housing, is comparatively high, or if local taxes are high, or if there is a competitor down the road... any number of things.

One thing is certain; you shouldn't select a field of study based primarily on an average starting salary number in a table. Your biggest kicks will come from doing work that is interesting, satisfying and fun for you. Since you have likely settled into an engineering program before ever having seen the data above, chances are that's the field that is most interesting to you. Don't worry about the money; doing good work always pays.

Over the past ten years or so, starting salaries in all engineering disciplines have risen substantially. In 2000, electrical engineers, for example, were typically offered salaries of about $46k. By 2005, starting salaries were up to the low $50k range. In 2008, a BSEE could expect to start in the mid $50k's, and as the chart above indicated, in 2009 the starting salary was averaging more than $60k.

Part Two: Earnings Growth

<u>The Experience Factor</u>

As you mature in your field, you can expect your salary to grow. Salaries increase for two reasons: your increasing maturity as an engineer makes you more valuable to your company and your raises

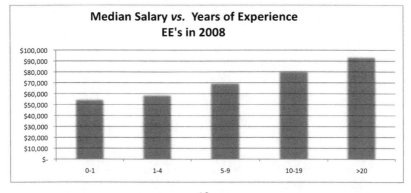

will reflect that fact; and the value of a dollar decreases (generally) due to inflation. There is no way to predict how your salary will grow over time. What we do have is data of salaries of engineers with different numbers of years of experience, paid during the same year. So, for example, a new BSEE employee in late 2008 had a nationally averaged median salary[2] of about $55k. That same year, electrical engineers with 1 to 4 years of experience were making $59k. Those with 5 to 9 years of experience were making $70k; 10 to 19 years — $81k; and engineers with 20 years or more of experience made $94k.

Don't confuse this trend with what *you* may earn over time. Extrapolating these data a bit, it looks like BS engineers with say 25 years of experience are likely to earn about twice what junior engineers make, on average, in 2008. However, it doesn't tell you how senior engineers' salaries increased over time. To get an idea of the increase in salary experienced by senior engineers over their professional lifetimes, you'd have to go back to 1983 and see what the average starting salary was then. Without a doubt, it would look pitifully small by today's standards. Why is that? Inflation of course. Over the past 50 years, the US rate of inflation, as measured by the Consumer Price Index[3], has varied from about 1% to over 13%! Back in 1985, for example, one dollar then could buy the goods and services that $2 buys in 2010. Back then, a salary of $25k would have been equivalent to a 2010 salary of $50k. At about 1975, a dollar would have been worth about $4 in 2010. In 1969, it would have been equivalent to about $6 in 2010 money. A yearly salary of $8,333 in 1969 would have bought what $50,000 would buy in 2010! So going back in time, or looking forward over the years, requires a more careful analysis than just a comparison of dollar for

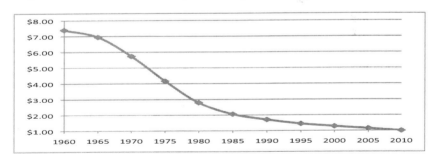

---

[2] Data obtained from www.payscale.com
[3] The CPI measures changes through time in the price level of a "market basket" of consumer goods and services purchased by households.

dollar. Take a look at this graph that shows the value of a dollar earned in prior years in terms of 2010 dollar purchasing power. As you can see, it's quite spectacular. Will the rather modest inflation rates of the past 10 years continue? No one knows. But if you're planning to sock away some resources for your future, keep inflation in mind.

Pros and Cons of Graduate School

Students often ask whether they should stay in school another year or two and get an MS, or an MBA degree, or go to work with a BS. What about a PhD? These are very important career-determining questions, and they deserve your attention.

Looking only at the salary data, the facts are clear. Engineers with an MS degree will be offered starting positions with significantly higher salaries, on average, than those with a BS degree. The differential again depends upon the specific field, location, the economic environment, etc. Say the difference between a starting MS and BS salary is 12% – 15%, a fairly typical range. If it takes you a year or two to get an MS after your BS, you may have given up two years of BS salary, not to mention the tuition costs. How long would it take to make that back as an MS-trained engineer? If the wage differential remained at that range forever, you might conclude that it would take a very long time to make up the lost pay and tuition costs. However, the data indicates that the wage differential increases consistently with increasing years of experience. It's pretty clear why this would be so. As an MS-degreed engineer, you are more valuable to a company, and because of the advanced training, your enhanced ability to learn more quickly and do more advanced tasks increases your value more rapidly than that of a BS-degreed engineer.

More important than the dollars, however, is the range of jobs that becomes available to engineers with advanced degrees. This diagram shows how a typical major corporation employing engineers fills its jobs at different levels with people having different academic credentials. Among the engineers, for example, 80% have BS degrees, 15% have MS degrees and a slim 5% have PhD degrees.

CEO
VPs
40% MS
60% PhD, MBA

DIRECTORS
DEPT. HEADS
SUPERVISORS
10% BS; 40% MS; 50% PhD

ENGINEERS
80% BS; 15% MS; 5% PhD

The middle management ranks are populated by 10% BS, 40% MS, and 50% PhDs. Upper management is generally 40% MS and 60% PhD or MBA or multiple degreed individuals. One can never know what opportunities may come your way over the course of one's career, but this figure certainly suggests that the best opportunities present themselves to those who get advanced degrees.

We shall return to the question of advanced degrees and how they may affect the direction of your career in Chapter Four, dealing with *The Corporate Enterprise.*

Continuing Education and Professional Growth

There is nothing more important to maintaining your employability and your value as an engineer than your commitment to continuing education. The pace of change in all fields of specialization is nothing less than astonishing. An engineer who relies on knowledge that becomes obsolete risks stagnation of earnings, or worse.

An article published in the Journal of Scientific & Industrial Research in 2006 reported the depreciation rates of technical knowledge for a wide range of industries. The analysis was based on the number of years for which patents are licensed by the various industries (see Chapter Six, Patents), which is an indicator of the number of years an innovative technology is useful before another replaces it. Here are the results:

Industry	Rate %	Industry	Rate %
Food & Beverage	11.87	Chemicals	13.10
Paper	12.02	Transport Equipment	13.71
Base Metal	12.62	Precision	13.92
Machinery	12.75	Electrical	14.39
Non-metallic Mineral	12.84	Electronics	16.08
Textile	13.09	Computer	16.79

Annual Technology Depreciation Rates

Thus, in the food and beverage or paper products industries, at the end of each year, on average, only about 88% of the most innovative technology is still useful. After the second year, 88% of 88% remains, and so forth. Thus, in those fields, the half-life of innovative technology, i.e., when 50% of the technology is no longer useful, works out to be 5.4 years. By contrast, in the computer industry, the half-life of innovation is 3.9 years! If you compare that result to the longevity of your last few laptops, you may see a similarity. In addition, the depreciation rates have been rising consistently over the years. The pace of obsolescence is accelerating.

There are no shortcuts here. You must constantly learn new things in order to maintain an optimum career potential. Fortunately, there are many avenues for continuing education. You may:

* Join your professional society.

* Subscribe to all the trade publications that are important in your discipline. Each of the professional societies produces excellent publications that range in level from the magazine style to the archival academic journal.

* Attend as many technical conferences as you can. Go to the trade shows, where new equipment and products will be displayed. Talk to the vendors and follow up with some research on the new technologies you have found.

* Inquire with your employer about the availability of programs that encourage you to get an advanced university degree. Many companies have tuition reimbursement benefits or will offer time off with pay while you are attending classes. Look for evening classes in your discipline.

The pace of innovation is increasing, and you may find that you cannot learn everything you might wish to know throughout the breadth of your discipline. As engineers mature in their fields, it is common to specialize and become expert in a few narrow areas. Select those areas carefully, with an eye toward the future. Avoid technological obsolescence at all costs.

Essay Questions:

1) Why did you choose your field of engineering? What do you hope to accomplish?

2) Is graduate school an attractive option for you? If you are undecided, what would help you decide? If you don't think it's for you, what might increase the chances of your getting an advanced degree?

3) If you know an older engineer, perhaps retired now, or perhaps one of the more senior professors in your department, ask them what their starting salary was, and what the year was. Don't laugh until after you leave the room. Then figure out the value of that salary in present-day dollars. Did society value engineers differently in the past than now?

Chapter Three

Societal Expectations of the Engineering Professional

IT IS NOT TITLES THAT HONOR MEN, BUT MEN THAT HONOR TITLES. ~ MACHIAVELLI

I recently went to a new doctor and noticed he was located in something called the Professional Building. I felt better right away.   - George Carlin

Part One: What is a Professional?

Why are doctors and lawyers, and people in certain other lines of work, thought of as being *professionals*? Most students asked that question think of the many years of schooling that a doctor or lawyer must have. Some suggest that people rely on them for help when they have problems, and therefore there is a great deal of trust placed in them to perform their work to the best of their abilities. A few point out that doctors have to pass a licensing exam, and lawyers have to pass the bar exam. The more cynical students point out that they both generally make lots of money.

It is valuable to look this up, and get an expert opinion. For example, a very complete definition[4] follows:

> A profession is a disciplined group of individuals who adhere to ethical standards and hold themselves out as, and are accepted by the public as possessing special knowledge and skills in a widely recognized body of learning derived from research, education and training at a high level, and who are prepared to apply this knowledge and exercise these skills in the interest of others.
>
> It is inherent in the definition of a profession that a code of ethics governs the activities of each profession. Such codes require behavior and practice beyond the personal moral obligations of an individual. They define and demand high standards of behavior in respect to the services provided to the public and in dealing with professional colleagues. Further, these

---

[4] Australian Council of Professions (British style of spelling was changed to American spelling). (http://www.professions.com.au/defineprofession.html). © Copyright Professions Australia 2010. Permission granted for republication.

codes are enforced by the profession and are acknowledged and accepted by the community.

So, the important points are lots of training, standards set and enforced by the profession itself, and ethical service to the public. How does engineering stack up against these criteria?

Surely, no engineering student would deny the huge commitment that must be made to acquire the education needed to be an engineer — Check. What about the rest of it?

You are also well aware of the professional society that is associated with your discipline: IEEE for electrical engineers, ASME for mechanical engineers, AIChE for chemical engineers, ASCE for civil engineers, etc. But do these organizations do anything more than publish journals? Did you know that each one has a *Code of Ethics*?

<u>Professional Codes of Ethics</u>

Let's go back a few years... 2,400 give or take a couple, and we find a physician by the name of Hippocrates practicing his art in Greece. He, or more likely one of his students, wrote a document now known as *The Hippocratic Oath*[5] that is still a basis of part of the graduation ceremonies of many medical schools. It is illuminating to read this document, presented below:

I swear by Apollo Physician and Asclepius and Hygieia and Panaceia and all the gods and goddesses, making them my witnesses, that I will fulfill according to my ability and judgment this oath and this covenant: To hold him who has taught me this art as equal to my parents and to live my life in partnership with him, and if he is in need of money to give him a share of mine, and to regard his offspring as equal to my brothers in

---

[5] Translated from the Greek by Ludwig Edelstein. From *The Hippocratic Oath: Text, Translation, and Interpretation*, by Ludwig Edelstein. Baltimore: Johns Hopkins Press, 1943.

male lineage and to teach them this art - if they desire to learn it - without fee and covenant; to give a share of precepts and oral instruction and all the other learning to my sons and to the sons of him who has instructed me and to pupils who have signed the covenant and have taken an oath according to the medical law, but no one else. I will apply dietetic measures for the benefit of the sick according to my ability and judgment; I will keep them from harm and injustice. I will neither give a deadly drug to anybody who asked for it, nor will I make a suggestion to this effect. Similarly I will not give to a woman an abortive remedy. In purity and holiness I will guard my life and my art. I will not use the knife, not even on sufferers from stone[6], but will withdraw in favor of such men as are engaged in this work. Whatever houses I may visit, I will come for the benefit of the sick, remaining free of all intentional injustice, of all mischief and in particular of sexual relations with both female and male persons, be they free or slaves. What I may see or hear in the course of the treatment or even outside of the treatment in regard to the life of men, which on no account one must spread abroad, I will keep to myself, holding such things shameful to be spoken about. If I fulfill this oath and do not violate it, may it be granted to me to enjoy life and art, being honored with fame among all men for all time to come; if I transgress it and swear falsely, may the opposite of all this be my lot.

Why is it important for engineers to read and think about this Oath?

This document is the world's first statement of the *ethical precepts* of a profession. In it, Hippocrates states that he will train his pupils, but only if they agree to these precepts. This is the beginning of the idea of *self-regulation* of the profession. In other words, each physician is responsible to insure that other physicians adhere to the high standards of the community of physicians. He pledges not to support suicide. Physicians and society are still debating that proposition! Some states permit doctor-assisted suicide, and some don't. He pledges not to support abortion, still an incredibly divisive topic these days. As a physician, and not a surgeon, he will practice the art he knows, but not

---

[6] This phrase refers to those suffering from kidney or gallstones, and as Hippocrates was a physician, not a surgeon, he pledged not to "use the knife" and perform an operation, but to leave that to those skilled in that art.

19

"use the knife", which is beyond his body of knowledge and skill. He will steer clear of inappropriate relations with his patients, and maintain professional boundaries. And, he pledges to maintain the confidentiality and privacy of his patients. It only took our society 2,400 years to codify that idea in the HIPAA Privacy Rule.[7] Isn't it amazing how "modern" were the ethical dilemmas that Hippocrates dealt with so long ago...

Each of the professional societies associated with the several engineering disciplines has adopted a Code of Ethics. The code for electrical engineers[8], for example, is reproduced below:

The IEEE Code of Ethics

We, the members of the IEEE, in recognition of the importance of our technologies in affecting the quality of life throughout the world, and in accepting a personal obligation to our profession, its members and the communities we serve, do hereby commit ourselves to the highest ethical and professional conduct and agree:

1. to accept responsibility in making decisions consistent with the safety, health and welfare of the public, and to disclose promptly factors that might endanger the public or the environment;

2. to avoid real or perceived conflicts of interest whenever possible, and to disclose them to affected parties when they do exist;

3. to be honest and realistic in stating claims or estimates based on available data;

4. to reject bribery in all its forms;

5. to improve the understanding of technology, its appropriate application, and potential consequences;

6. to maintain and improve our technical competence and to undertake technological tasks for others only if qualified by

---

[7] HIPAA stands for *The Health Insurance Portability and Accountability Act of 1996*, and you sign a statement at every doctor's office that you visit acknowledging that you were informed how your physician maintains the confidentiality of your records.

[8] Approved by the IEEE Board of Directors, February 2006; www.ieee.org/membership_services/membership/ethics_code.html

training or experience, or after full disclosure of pertinent limitations;

7. to seek, accept, and offer honest criticism of technical work, to acknowledge and correct errors, and to credit properly the contributions of others;

8. to treat fairly all persons regardless of such factors as race, religion, gender, disability, age, or national origin;

9. to avoid injuring others, their property, reputation, or employment by false or malicious action;

10. to assist colleagues and co-workers in their professional development and to support them in following this code of ethics.

The codes for other professional engineering disciplines have many of the same elements. On first reading, this code seems perfectly reasonable. There are a few issues that surface with a little more thought, however. For example, precept #1 says that electrical engineers shall accept responsibility in making decisions consistent with the safety, health and welfare of the public. The word *responsibility* has quite a few meanings, but in this context, I take this phrase to mean *moral obligation.* Does it only apply to *decisions?* What about recommendations? The phrase *to disclose promptly* seems OK at first, but if you were in a situation such as this, *to whom* are you supposed to disclose the endangering factors? The public at large? The government? Your client? And what if only a few individuals, but *not* your client, would be endangered. Do you disclose your concerns to those individuals at risk, perhaps against your client's best interests? If you do disclose a dangerous situation to your client, and your client doesn't do anything about it, is your responsibility, your *moral obligation,* satisfied? Or are you in a worse fix? Just asking...

In precept #2, the phrase *conflict of interest* is often not understood. The term requires a good understanding of what *interest* means. For example, one may assume that you have an *interest* in maintaining your health. You have an *interest* in getting good grades, in making a good living, in all sorts of *personal* desirable factors in your life. Of course, we all have our own set of interests. If you accepted a job from a client, only to find that in doing that job to the best of your ability, you might, in some way, go against your *own* personal interests, then you have a *conflict of interests.* Here's an example. You own a home in town. You are hired by the electric power utility in that area as a consultant, to recommend the best route for a new high voltage electric distribution line. The cheapest and most direct route would be right through your neighborhood. The company is prepared to buy up all the necessary property, bulldoze the right-of-way and build the line. You don't want to move, you like your neighbors, you like where you're living, etc. Bingo. Conflict of interest. Your personal interests are in conflict with the economic interests of your client.

Conflicts of interest may be less obvious than that. If, instead of your home, one of your favorite pizza stores was located in that neighborhood, you still might not want to recommend that the most economical line be built through the neighborhood, simply out of loyalty to the store's owners, or your aversion to finding another place to buy pizza. Whenever you have a personal reason that could sway your judgment away from the best advice you could otherwise give to your client, you have a conflict of interest. Precept #2 says you must endeavor to avoid getting into such situations. Sometimes they are inevitable and unavoidable. If that is the case, transparency is the only solution. You must disclose the fact that you have a conflict to everyone who may be involved, and then, if your client says, well do your best anyway, at least your client will know that your advice may be tainted by your conflict. Your client may ask someone else for a second opinion. At least, all the facts are disclosed, so that good decisions can be made and there aren't any hidden agendas.

Part Two: When Do *You* Become a Professional?

While you are studying your way towards your BS degree, your thoughts of "being a professional" are likely to be quite far from your mind. Some of you may have heard of the "PE" exam, which is a very comprehensive two-part licensing exam given by the National Council of Examiners for Engineering and Surveying. If you pass that, you can add "PE" (Professional Engineer) after your name. That's not what I mean, however. (Just to clean this up a bit, the PE *license* is awarded under the regulation of each state, and is generally required only of engineers who are in charge of work on public projects, and do such things as stamp (verify) such designs, bid for government contracts, and otherwise offer services to the public. It is more relevant to civil engineers, for example, than to computer engineers.) No, I am thinking about your becoming a "professional" in the sense that Hippocrates would understand: learning those special, highly-technical skills that characterize your discipline, and accepting and supporting the Code of

Ethics that defines your responsibilities to society, thereby joining the community of your engineering colleagues. Does all this happen in a flash as someone hands you your diploma? Maybe when you get your first real job? Maybe when you get your first paycheck? I'm not sure, frankly, but what I *am* sure about is that it doesn't happen in a flash.

The problem is that for most of your life, you have been a student. That's good; don't get me wrong! But some students have a certain set of "attitudes" about things, like — getting the homework done in the least possible time, or not worrying about not quite getting it done; or borrowing a friend's lab report, just this once; or memorizing something because you just don't have the time right now to fully understand it; or _____ (fill in the blank).

Let's face it — these are *not* professional behaviors. Copying someone's lab report is not quite in line with properly crediting the contributions of others, which you may recognize as part of precept #7 of the IEEE Code. The point is, it takes time and effort and commitment to change behaviors and attitudes. It can't be done in a flash. No matter where you fall in the spectrum of students, from really committed to lackadaisical, *now* is your time, as a student, to work toward acquiring the attitudes of a professional. Society expects its professional engineers to be accurate, correct, complete, totally trust-worthy. It is clear, I hope, that those that lack a truly professional attitude about working to the highest possible standards *as students* are simply delaying the time when they can acquire the skills necessary to be independent, fully-competent professional engineers. Getting your degree isn't the criterion. If you graduate with gaps in your understanding, technical details you should know but are still a little fuzzy about, you're not there yet. If you start your first job with an attitude of "it's good enough," you will be in for a few rough years. Start making that crucial transition now. Think of yourself as a professional *future* engineer, and suffuse everything you do with a truly professional attitude. It will take you some time to develop that kind of self-discipline, but it will help you immensely.

Essay Questions

1) Describe an ethical dilemma or conflict of interest that occurred in your life, and how it was resolved.

2) Some colleges have a student-run Board of Ethics to enforce the school's student code. If you were in such a school and saw a fellow student cheating on a test, under what circumstances would you report it or not, and why?

3) Describe how you personally feel about your transition from student to professional.

4) In what ways do the precepts of a code of ethics differ from law?

5) You are employed by a geotechnical engineering firm. The city hired your firm to assess the possible instability of a hillside that they own. You find that the hillside was in great danger of sliding and recommend that drain lines be installed immediately to remove as much water from the slope as possible. Before the city can get that work done, the hill collapses and damages homes below. The homeowners sue your company[9] because you didn't tell them about the danger. Should you have? The homeowners' suit relied on a state law that provides that engineers have a duty to "safeguard life, health, property and to promote the public welfare," a statement similar to the first principles in most engineering codes of ethics.

6) Distracted drivers account for over 20% of injury crashes. The greatest source of driver distraction is use of a wireless device.

   Discuss: should engineers design vehicles with built-in GPS devices, or would this be an action inconsistent with the safety, health and welfare of the public?

---

[9] See for example caselaw.findlaw.com/wa-court-of-appeals/1340399.html

Chapter Four
The Corporate Enterprise

Honesty is the single most important factor having a direct bearing on the final success of an individual, corporation, or product. – Ed McMahon

A criminal is a person with predatory instincts who has not sufficient capital to form a corporation.
- Howard Scott

Part One: Company Characteristics

The Business Corporation

A corporation is a business organization that is regulated by the laws of each state, and given certain rights and responsibilities, much as if it were a real person. A corporation can own property, pay taxes, sign binding contracts, employ others to work for it, sue other corporations or individuals, even have its own credit rating, etc. All of these rights and responsibilities are distinct and separate from the rights and responsibilities of the members of the corporation, who are its owners or shareholders. An important aspect of corporate law is the concept of *limited liability*. If the corporation gets into financial or legal trouble, the corporation can go bankrupt, or it can be sued and forced to pay a fine, but the shareholders can lose no more than their investment in the corporation. Shareholders, as a rule, are not legally responsible for the actions of the corporation. The corporation also has perpetual life. If successful, it can accumulate property even as its owners come and go. This feature permits corporations to get very rich and powerful, some with assets well over $100 billion and employing hundreds of thousands of people worldwide. These assets are not owned by the shareholders, but by the corporation itself. The shareholders, as a group, own the corporation, each one owning a fraction in proportion to the number of shares owned. A corporation can decide to dissolve itself ("die") and liquidate its assets to its creditors and shareholders, or it may be dissolved by court action. The oldest corporation in existence today was started in Sweden, in 1347![10]

---

[10] Stora Kopparberg ("Great Copper Mountain"), originally a Swedish copper mining company, was granted a charter from King Magnus IV of Sweden in 1347, with miners and the Bishop of Västerås owning shares in the enterprise. It closed the mine that had produced copper since the tenth century, and is now the world's second largest pulp and paper manufacturer (Stora Enso).

25

Corporations are run by a chief executive officer (CEO) who is selected by a board of directors, each one of which is in turn elected by the shareholders to represent their interests.

Corporations can be public or private. The distinction is based on the rules governing the purchase and transfer of the shares, or stock, of the corporation. The shares of a private corporation are held by a group of individuals, and cannot be sold to anyone outside that group except by consent of the shareholders themselves. On the other hand, shares of a public corporation may be traded, bought and sold by anyone, and stock markets have developed to facilitate the exchange of these shares. Because the public needs to know if the shares of a public corporation might be a good investment, these corporations are required to publish yearly financial reports and disclose a great deal of other information. Such disclosures are not required of private corporations.

Non-corporate Business Organizations

A single individual may own a business, which would be called a sole proprietorship. Similarly, a group of individuals may reach an agreement to own a business as a general partnership. Neither of these simple designations implies any form of limited liability. The owners would be responsible for all the debts of the company, as the company has no separate legal status. Why would the owner(s) of a company choose to accept the risk inherent in these non-corporate structures? The simple answer is that the corporate laws of each state make many demands on the corporation. A corporation must submit many legal documents to the state, such as Articles of Incorporation and a set of Bylaws, which describe how the corporation will be organized and managed. Lawyers need to be hired to make sure the corporation is in compliance with all the rules; accountants are generally needed to calculate how much tax the corporation owes; an annual meeting of the shareholders must be held at which the chief executive officer describes what has happened in the business over the course of the previous year, etc. For some business owners, the limited liability afforded by a corporation doesn't justify the extra hassle.

Several other structures are permitted by the law, such as limited liability partnerships, limited liability companies, limited partnerships, etc., These are hybrid organizations, in between general partnerships and corporations, and are often the preferred organization structures used by groups of lawyers, architects, physicians, etc.

The Start-Up

Anyone can start a company, and organize it according to any of the structures mentioned above. If you are interested in starting your own company at some point in the future, there is much to learn, and you should think about taking some courses in business administration and finance. If you are interested in working for a start-up technical company, you should be aware of the risks. A large fraction of start-ups fail, and lose a great deal of money that had been invested in them by business associates and venture capitalists.[11] You may be offered the opportunity to accept part of your pay in stock options, which may become valueless. Your job at a start-up has no security, and although it may be a thrilling place to work, you may not be working there for long. On the other hand, employees hired in the early days of a start-up business that becomes successful may find themselves owning stock worth a great deal, and rising to high executive levels in the organization as the company grows. We have all heard these fabulous success stories but keep in mind, they constitute a tiny minority.

Part Two: Who Owns GE?

The General Electric Company, GE, began in 1892 as a merger of two small companies, one of which was owned by Thomas Edison. Now, GE is the quintessential multifaceted multinational engineering corporation, employing about 300,000 people in over 100 countries, and they're still making light bulbs! If you were one of the hundreds of thousands of engineers employed by a large corporation such as GE, wouldn't you like to know who's calling the shots at the top?

So who owns GE, for example? There are more than 10 billion shares of GE common stock out there, owned by more than 5 million shareholders, making it the most widely held public corporation in the world.

How do the 17 members of the Board of Directors of GE represent all these 5 million shareholders? It seems like a hard thing to

---

[11] According to the National Venture Capital Association, the majority of venture capital is invested in high-risk, high technology companies including software, biotechnology, medical devices, media and entertainment, wireless communications, internet, and networking. They estimate that 40% of venture backed companies fail, 40% have moderate returns, and only 20% or less produce high returns.

do. Clearly the major shareholders would have, and probably should have, a larger voice in the governance of this corporation. They have a lot at stake. So who are these major shareholders? The table below shows the ten largest shareholders of GE common stock as of 2010, and the fraction of all the outstanding shares that they own.

HOLDER	%
The Vanguard Group Inc.	3.56
State Street Corporation	3.41
BlackRock Institutional Trust Company, N.A.	2.65
FMR LLC	1.66
Northern Trust Corporation	1.48
Dodge & Cox Inc.	1.28
Bank of New York Mellon Corporation	1.23
Wellington Management Company, LLP	1.22
Vanguard Total Stock Market Index Fund	1.05
T. Rowe Price Associates Inc.	0.96
TOTAL:	18.50

Of the 17 board members in 2010, in addition to the CEO of GE, 12 were either CEOs or past CEOs of major corporations in very diverse industries, three were at universities, and one was a former US Senator. This is a very typical board composition for a major corporation. The business experiences and world views of such a group of highly accomplished individuals would be a huge asset to any company trying to maneuver through the complexities of today's global economy. Can these board members represent the interests of the millions of stockholders? I leave it to you to decide.

Part Three: The Engineering Career Path

As you contemplate your career as an engineer, you should think about what you might like to be doing ten or twenty years down the road. Some wise fellow (or was he a wise guy) once said, "Failing to plan is the same as planning to fail." The truth is, a good engineer starting off on the lowest rung of the career ladder has unlimited opportunities. The chart on the next page lays out the main directions in which your career could go. I should point out that each company would have its own titles, and they may not be identical to the titles in the chart. In addition, small companies would not have as many subcategories as shown in this figure.

The first part of your career path would likely take you up through higher levels of competency as an engineer. Starting at the Engineer level, you can expect promotions over time up through the ranks, depending on your performance. Senior engineers might have small groups of engineers working under their supervision. The Principal Engineer and Senior Principal Engineer would be given more and more independent responsibility. They may be called department heads or directors. Most engineers are content to remain somewhere in this track. Above the level of Senior Principal Engineer, there are four significantly distinct directions in which your career may move. The four columns represent roles with varying degrees of technical focus (far left) and business focus (far right).

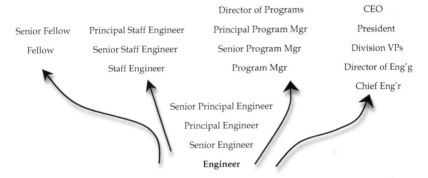

Some large companies have a Fellows track. Fellows generally have a PhD degree, and do either basic research that might lead to new products, new technologies, improved efficiency, etc., or are called upon to solve complex technical problems that occur in the company. In some companies, the Fellow designation is an honorary title, and the Fellow usually is a high level manager as well. For example, Intel has designated about 50 Fellows throughout the company, selected on the basis of their technical leadership and outstanding contributions to the company and the industry.

The role of Staff Engineer is a little closer to the business side of the company. For example, a Staff Engineer may be asked to help flesh out the high-level technical details of new products, perhaps proposed by the marketing department. You might imagine an automobile manufacturing company, where the marketing department decides that a new high-end luxury car would be a great new product, and wants to know what new whiz-bang technology could be featured, like a collision-avoidance system, or a super smooth suspension with active feedback... Staff Engineers might be deciding what would be possible given the state of the technology, and what it might cost.

Still closer to the business side of the company is the Program Manager track. Here we find people who are directly responsible for managing all the elements of getting a product to market, including its detailed design and manufacture. They might be involved in making sure their design group is successful in meeting all the specifications, that the product can be manufactured within the allotted budget, that it passes all quality control tests, etc. To be sure, they are managers, and don't do all this work themselves. Their role is to make sure the work gets done by the engineers and analysts that work for them.

On the far right are the business managers, who deal with major budget issues, profitability, facilities planning and acquisition, mergers with other companies, taxes, and financing the operation of the company as a whole. Many people in these positions would have training in business administration or economics, and have significant financial experience. However, in an engineering company, you will also find many people in these positions that started out with an engineering degree. Where would you like to end up?

Part Four: Corporate Structures and the Org Chart

One of the first documents you may be handed by someone in the human resource department on your first day of work is a diagram of the structure of your company (the organization chart, or org chart). It attempts to show the various components of the company, who does what, relative levels of responsibility, the chain of command, etc. If you were to try to locate yourself on that chart, you'd undoubtedly be very near the bottom, with layer upon layer of ~~turtles~~ supervisors, department heads, directors and vice presidents above you. Oh well, you have to start somewhere.

It's turtles

all the way down

30

In all seriousness, though, there is a great deal to be learned about the company from its org chart, and what you learn may give you an indication of how you will be asked to work. For example, companies that employ large numbers of engineers generally structure themselves in one of two principal ways. The first is called Product-Oriented Organization. The second is called Functional-Matrix Organization.

Product-Oriented Organization

A schematic org chart for a product-oriented organization is shown below for an automobile company. In this structure, three different products are being developed simultaneously. Each of these projects is headed by a product manager, who communicates with the upper management of the company through the program manager. The program manager is in contact with the marketing department and staff engineers, where the general specifications for the product are defined.

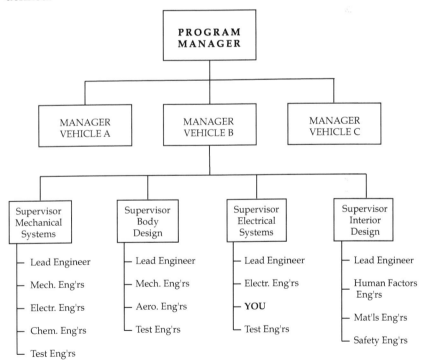

The program manager deals with marketing issues, budgets of all the product development projects, in this case, vehicles A, B and C, making sure the product managers have the resources they need, etc. The manager of the "vehicle B" product sets the schedule for completion of each aspect of the development of that product, decides how the budget for the project shall be divided among the various activities, organizes the teams that work on the project, evaluates the progress of each team, coordinates the activities of each team and makes sure they are working toward the common goal. Project managers have budgetary oversight; therefore they must approve salary distributions for members of their projects, new hires, promotions, etc.

Let us imagine that you are an engineer in the electrical systems group. Your supervisor will assign specific tasks to you and tell you when they need to be completed. Your progress will be monitored, and your supervisor will make sure you have the tools you need to do your job. You will get feedback during semiannual or annual personnel review meetings. Your supervisor will report to the project manager about your strengths and weaknesses, and recommend you for raises and promotion.

The main advantages of this type of organization, from your standpoint, is the fact that you report to one person who is very familiar with your work, and can readily appreciate your accomplishments. That same person recommends you for raises and promotion. Remember that supervisors' most important personnel responsibilities are to make their teams look good, and to get their people promoted. After all, your supervisor may have recommended hiring you, and if your team is successful, your supervisor looks good too. Your supervisor's goals are therefore in line with your own.

The overall scheme of a product-oriented organization leads to a shared sense of accomplishment when the product is successful, and a sharing in the rewards of success. In later years, you will still be associated in the eyes of upper management with a successful project. You will also be working in a very interdisciplinary environment. Within your own group are engineers with different backgrounds, and you may become the local expert in your specific discipline. That reputation also sticks with you. You will get respect and recognition for your successes.

The potential disadvantages of this organization are also quite apparent. If the product is a failure, you may be out of a job. All the other projects may have all the people they need, and unless your company is very large, with new projects coming along all the time, your company may not have any work for you to do. At a minimum, you may be labeled as being a member of a failed project. It need not have been your fault. The product could have failed because of market forces, or decisions made higher up in the company about costs or features. Welcome to the real world...

Even if your product is a rousing success, be prepared for a major change. Your electrical systems team, in fact the entire group working on vehicle B, will be redeployed to work on another product. Hopefully. Part of upper management's responsibility is to plan how to wind down one project and time the start of others so that there is a continuity of work, and a minimum of employee dissatisfaction. And even though you may have become the local expert on your niche technology as applied to vehicle B, the next product may require entirely new approaches, new ideas, and a whole range of different problems to solve. It's important for you to be successful on a sequence of products. That gives your managers confidence in your ability to solve a wide range of problems and puts you on the path toward promotion to supervisory and management responsibilities.

The Functional-Matrix Organization

You may find an entirely different structure in your company. The chart on the next page shows the basic features of the functional-matrix organization. The functional groups are the horizontal rows of the matrix. The columns represent individuals working on three different product lines. Let us say that you are again among the EEs working on vehicle B. In this organization, your tasks on that project would be assigned by the program manager of vehicle B. However, your personnel review is the responsibility of the manager of electrical systems, on the left of this chart. Coordination between the program managers and the managers of the functional groups is essential in this structure. A program manager in need of a particular type of engineer for a particular job has to go to the functional manager and request that an appropriate engineer be assigned to the project. When that job is completed, the engineer is released back to the pool of engineers managed by the functional manager, and may be assigned to another project.

There is a constant flow of engineers between projects as the needs of these projects change. In a large organization, this structure has great efficiency. Engineers are placed where there is work to be done. It is the responsibility of the director of engineering to make sure that each of the managers has enough people to meet the needs of all the projects, but not too large a surplus. This planning is done by consultation with the director of programs, who knows what projects will be coming on line, and what their budgets and timetables are likely to be.

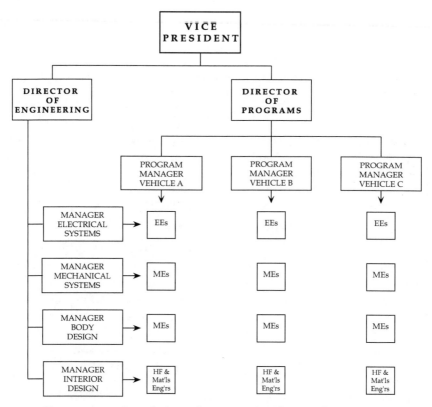

From your point of view, there are significant advantages in this type of organization. In the first place, you will be working on a variety of projects over time. This can be an opportunity for you to broaden your skill set and see a larger picture of your profession and of the company. It may be more interesting to move from project to project than to stay in one program from beginning to end. If you happen to find yourself stuck on a problem, there are experts in your functional group who have probably encountered a similar problem before, and can advise you how to proceed. They may be sitting at the desks next to yours. Your functional manager is a resource as well. You may be interacting with other kinds of engineers in a vertical direction in your project, in order to make sure the interfaces between systems work smoothly, but the primary interaction will be horizontal, between members of your own discipline.

This structure also has some disadvantages. First of all, you have two bosses to please. They will be communicating constantly about how you are doing on your tasks, and it may be unclear at times who has the upper hand in reviewing your work. Your program manager may not be an engineer in your field, and may not have an appreciation of the difficulties of the tasks assigned to you. There is a potential disconnect here, with you in the middle. In addition, it may be harder to stand out in the crowd. All the engineers in your functional group are doing the same thing, moving from project to project, solving similar problems. The only one who gets any specific credit for a successful program is the program manager (who may also get the axe for a failed project). In a sense, the engineers are shielded from that risk, and from the associated rewards.

Which structure is best? It depends on the company. Every company has its own interpretation of these organizational structures. There are many variables, and many modifications. The two templates presented above are the extremes in a continuous array of possibilities. The structure chosen for a manufacturing company may be a very poor one for a software company. A huge corporation may have many different styles of organization for its different business elements. In any company, your approach that will have the best potential for your success will include the following:

- ❖ Always give your job 100%. Your manager's assessments of you and comparisons between you and your peers are unavoidable. You simply must strive for excellence and professionalism at all times.

- ❖ Map out the chain of command from your position up to the vice president above you. Try to understand what these jobs entail. Find out what your managers did especially well to achieve their promotions. This will give you some insight into what your company most values in it employees.

- ❖ Find your job description and the job description of the position above yours. Make sure you meet all aspects of your job description. Work to acquire skills that meet the requirements of the next level up.

Part Five: Employee Loyalty

Without any doubt, the upper management of any company would love to improve the loyalty of employees. A key measure of employee loyalty is the employee turnover rate. Companies that have a high turnover of excellent workers have to expend significant resources to recruit and then train replacements, and suffer lost productivity during that entire period. If those employees would only stay longer, management's job would be so much easier!

Business consultants have recorded a striking change in employee attitudes over the years. Today's employees are much more loyal to their own life goals than to the goals of their employers. This was not true for the parents and grandparents of today's workers. How many of you might have seen the gold watch given to your grandfather on the 25th anniversary of his employment with his company? There are many such heirloom gold watches, wrapped in little felt bags, and put away with the mementos of days long gone.

Do employees owe their employers their loyalty? After all, they are getting a good salary, benefits, retirement accounts... It may be useful to think about employee loyalty using the same criteria as we apply to other kinds of loyalty. You are loyal to your friends and to your family. Why? Because you know that if you were in trouble, they would be there for you, and you would be there for them. There is an almost guaranteed reciprocity.

During the economic downturn of 2008-9, about 5 million jobs were lost in the US. Job losses in engineering occurred most profoundly in specialties related to the construction industry, which was hard hit. Other disciplines faired very well by comparison. A great deal of the loyalty issue has to do with the size of the company, and personal commitment and rapport between managers and workers. There are many examples of small engineering companies asking their workers to take major pay cuts, go to 4 work days/week and other money-saving solutions so that the company could survive and retain the maximum possible number of employees. But if the work evaporates, there is little that a business owner can do.

In the world of large corporations, however, loyalty seems out of place. If a company is doing poorly, employees may lose their jobs. CEOs looking at the bottom line and hoping to satisfy their shareholders issue directives to their VPs to cut budgets by a non-negotiable percentage, and the pain gets passed down the line.

During good economic periods, if employee retention could be improved, everybody wins. Reduced turnover increases efficiency, makes the company more profitable, possibly affecting salary increases or bonuses, and increases the strength of relationships between employees. When employees are eager to be helpful to one another, the company benefits. The best companies understand that by aligning corporate policies with employee's life goals, employee retention is enhanced. The corporate policies that work best are those that

- ❖ reward employees for excellence, through bonuses, merit raises and appropriate promotion;

- ❖ encourage employees to take on increasing responsibility as they demonstrate their capabilities;

- ❖ make continuing education a company priority, through time off with pay, educational grants, bonuses for advanced degrees or other mechanisms.

If your company has these progressive policies, then there is much less to gain by looking for a new job every few years. If not, then keep your résumé up to date, and your eyes open for better opportunities, with no tinge of guilt for being disloyal. Remember, you are being paid for your work, and you owe your company no more than what you get in return.

Part Six: Ethics on the Job

As an engineer, you are bound by a code of ethics that distinguishes you as a member of an elite community of professionals. Let us imagine that you are working for a large corporation. Does your company also have a code of ethics? In most cases, the answer is yes. Corporate codes of ethics or codes of conduct can usually be found on company websites, and are always part of the orientation information given to new employees. If your company has a code of conduct, you'll hear about it. These codes are developed by the company itself, perhaps by the Board of Directors, or by a committee appointed by the CEO, and then approved by the Board.

Realistically, one has only to read the newspapers to find, seemingly on a daily basis, evidence that companies don't always hold to their own ethical standards. Consider the scenarios presented below, and choose a course of action that you think you would follow were the situation to unfold around you. You may come up with a course of action beyond what is suggested.

Exxon Mobil *vs* Global Warming

You're an environmental engineer with a BS in chemical engineering. Your job[12] at Exxon Mobil is to

* *Develop and execute plans for integrating environmental engineering design considerations and criteria into the development and execution of major projects;*

* *Investigate new technology and recommend application to provide longer-term cost-effective environmental benefits; be the repository of this technology and promote transfer within the company.*

You learn that Exxon Mobil was supporting[13] the Competitive Enterprise Institute, which was known for its aggressive campaigns that claimed that global warming was a fake. You find this extremely disturbing because your research tells you that global warming is real and dangerous, and referring to the Code of Ethics of AIChE, you see this statement, *"Members of the American Institute of Chemical Engineers shall uphold and advance the integrity, honor and dignity of the engineering profession by ... using their knowledge and skill for the enhancement of human welfare."*

What would you do? Here are some possibilities:

* You talk to your supervisor, who tells you, among other things, "if you don't like the company's policies, you can always quit." You promptly resign.

* After getting a lecture from your supervisor, you decide to shut up and stay.

* You write a letter to the CEO, noting Exxon Mobil's published Code of Conduct[14] (that states in part: *"Exxon Mobil Corporation encourages employees to ask questions, voice concerns, and make appropriate suggestions regarding the business practices of the Corporation"*), offering to set up a workshop including environmentalists and CEI, to explore the problem.

---

[12] Actual job description offered at Exxon Mobil Chemical Co., Baytown, TX.

[13] Exxon's funding of CEI, based on data released by the company itself, totaled over $2,000,000 since 1998.

[14] www.exxonmobil.com/

38

- You write a letter to the newspaper accusing the company of being unethical. You expect you'll be fired when you're found out.

Drug Contamination at GlaxoSmithKline

You are an industrial engineer at a huge drug manufacturing plant in Puerto Rico, owned by GlaxoSmithKline. You become aware of some slipshod practices at the plant that you think have resulted in significant contamination of many drugs produced there. Do you:

- Report the problem to your supervisor?

- Write a long report detailing the problem and send it to the company's chief engineer?

- Report your concerns to the Food and Drug Administration?

Alleged Faulty Flares at ATK Thiokol

You're an engineer working at ATK Thiokol, a very large military and aerospace contractor. They make a flare, a three-foot long, almost 5" diameter aluminum tube packed with rocket fuel, and designed to be dropped on parachutes over battlefields at night to light up the sky for several minutes, permitting observation of enemy movements. You suspect that the flares were using a faulty firing mechanism, and that the company knew they could be set off if dropped from five feet off the ground, for example if they were mishandled during transport. These flares burn at more than 3,600°F, which would melt steel. They were being sold under a specification that claimed they would be safe if dropped from ten feet. What would you do?

- Tell your boss?

- Tell the newspaper?

- Suggest that the company stop selling these flares to the US Army and start selling them to the Taliban?

Discussion of Ethical Dilemmas

The Exxon Mobil scenario is made up. However, it is a fact that Exxon Mobil employs large numbers of environmental engineers, and that from about 1998 through 2005, the Exxon Mobil Foundation contributed over $2 million to CEI. The unhappy employee is invented, but certainly could have existed. Problems such as this are *personal*, not *ethical.* It is not unethical for someone to believe that vast numbers of environmental scientists are making a mistake, that they are misinterpreting data, or that human activity does not make the earth warmer. It may be akin to the proverbial ostrich sticking his head in the sand (they don't, by the way), but it's not illegal and it's not unethical to hold those positions. The unhappy employee could quit, for sure, but I would imagine that after a few months without a job, the level of unhappiness would increase!

The case of the drug contamination at GlaxoSmithKline is true. It was not an industrial engineer, but the company's quality control manager that documented the pervasive contamination problem. She repeatedly told her management about the problems, but the company did nothing and fired her instead[15]. She then filed suit against her former employer. A federal law, called the False Claims Act, may be invoked by any person who claims that products were sold to the government under false claims (such as, in this case, contaminated drugs that were paid for by the government under Medicare and Medicaid). If the case seems solid, the federal government may join the suit, and any fine levied by the court against the defendant will be shared with the informer, legally called *the relator*, or more colloquially, the whistle-blower, up to 20%! In the Glaxo settlement, a fine of $750 million was ordered, and the former quality control manager's share was a cool $96 million!

In spite of the example described above, "blowing the whistle" on a corporation is fraught with difficulties. In the first place, unless a faulty product was sold to the United States government, there is no uniform law to protect the informer from the extraordinary expense of litigation and likely retaliation by the company. Each state has its own laws dealing with such issues. The laws of some states are extremely pro-business, and those of other states are less so. Requirements for evidence are uniformly high. The informer must have incontrovertible evidence of fraud or some other activity that must fall within the range of illegal acts covered by the laws of the state. Only an attorney can assess the chances of success of a suit, and advise on the economic

---

[15] Quoting from GSK's Code of Ethics: "GSK is committed to the highest standards of conduct in all aspects of its business. It is GSK's policy that its business is always carried on with honesty and integrity, and in compliance with all applicable legal and regulatory requirements."

risks to the whistle-blower. And then there are the personal and psychological traumas of a long and contentious trial (the Glaxo suit took 7 years to be resolved), coupled with a possibly prolonged period of unemployment. Under no circumstances should an employee steal documents to try to uncover evidence or disclose the sordid tale to the media before consulting with a knowledgeable attorney. Whistle-blowers who lose their cases or never get to trial because of their own unwitting acts that sabotage their legal positions, may find it impossible to get another job in their industry or profession. This is a very serious matter that must be handled with the utmost care. Get the advice of a lawyer before you do anything!

The case of the alleged faulty flares is also real. As of late 2010, the case had not yet come to trial. The government joined the case, and pointed to its $100 million contract with ATK to buy these devices. This is another situation in which the False Claims Act may be invoked. Perhaps by the time you read this, the case will have concluded. Look it up[16]. Did the government and the informer win or lose?

Part Seven: Working for the Government

The federal government employs[17] large numbers of engineers at locations all over the country and abroad. In 2010, over 43,000 professional engineers worked for US government agencies. Categories include electronics engineering, civil engineering and mechanical engineering. An almost equal number of general engineers (typically having a BA degree, not a BS) and engineering technicians are also employed. The employing agencies include the Departments of Defense, Transportation, Agriculture, Interior, Energy, Veterans Affairs, NASA and the EPA. There are also 17 major National Laboratories where state of the art research is pursued.

A former federal government human resources manager and consultant with over 30 years of experience described his perceptions of government employment. I present his excellent article here.

---

[16] Search: *ATK, flares, litigation*

[17] www.makingthedifference.org/federalcareers/engineering.shtml

Working for the Government[18]
Is Uncle Sam the Right Employer for You?

By David Hornestay

The challenge and mission of a federal agency can be exciting; the politics and bureaucracy can be frustrating. Placement and preparation have to be right.

Surveys tell us that most college seniors don't think seriously about working for the U.S. government. While Uncle Sam spends considerable dollars trying to interest "the best and the brightest" in federal careers, his efforts are up against both stereotypes and realities. Careful analysis, however, suggests that the right agency can provide a rewarding experience to many of today's job-seekers.

Unfortunately, first contacts with a government agency can provide a lifetime turnoff. Paying taxes or getting a student loan is likely to involve multiple forms, dense instructions, and a resource person who may be neither polite nor informative. Security checks at airports following 9/11 have only increased this potential for irritation. Movies, comedians, and the press fortify unfavorable impressions with revelations or comments on clumsiness, waste, and wrongdoing in government. Occasional worthwhile achievements like detecting and heading off epidemics or exploring a neighboring planet are attributed to atypical public servants who rise above bureaucratic obstacles.

Then, too, there are positive incentives for working in the private sector. While earning capacity in areas like finance, law, and medicine is foremost for many, there are other attractions like entrepreneurship and creative pursuits outside the government's scope.

But the clearly ineffective federal recruiting efforts have left most college students with little idea of the challenge and variety of work across many organizations and occupations. While the public has an idea of what FBI and CIA agents do, how many have any idea about cutting-edge research in agriculture and aeronautics leading to the food and aircraft of the future? How many might be interested in opportunities to actually make the government more efficient by working on the vast computer systems that impact and sometimes bedevil our daily lives?

The government has done a few things in recent years, typically not well publicized, to make itself a more attractive employer. The retirement

---

system, now including social security and a 401K type plan, has been made more compatible with private employment. This makes it possible to spend a few years with Uncle Sam without a lifetime commitment. Entry level salaries, supplemented by college loan repayments and recruitment bonuses, are comparable for most private occupations, with obvious exceptions like finance and top-tier law.

On the other hand, red tape, resource instability due to changing Administration and Congressional priorities, and targeting of agencies, programs, and individuals for attack by political figures are still day-to-day realities.

Agency web sites and contacts make it possible for a career-seeking person to find out whether a particular government office or program is right for him or her. In many cases, it would be worthwhile to fire up a search engine for a little research.

* * * * *

In general, only US citizens and nationals (residents of American Samoa and Swains Island) may work for the federal government in what is called the *competitive civil service*. Applicants for jobs in the competitive civil service must compete for placement with other applicants under a strictly defined merit system. There are a few exceptions that permit non-citizens to be employed, such as the unavailability of a citizen to fill the post, but this is a rare occurrence.

The organizational structure of the US government is exceedingly complex and confusing. However, following Mr. Hornestay's suggestion, if you are interested in looking at the types of jobs available in the civil service, your should check out

http://www.usajobs.gov/

the official site operated by the US Office of Personnel Management. This site makes job hunting across the entire breadth of the federal government relatively easy, permitting you to specify job key words and preferred geographical locations.

Essay Questions

1. Should a corporation have a social responsibility? Research the pros and cons of this issue. Consider especially Nobel Prize winner Milton Friedman's famous essay[19], *The Social Responsibility of Business is to Increase its Profits,"* and the many responses to it that present alternate views.

2. Check out the web site of a major corporation and find out what the company is doing in a socially responsible way. Why do some corporations spend money for these activities?

3. Find a recent whistle-blowing case in the news. Research the story and report on what the informer did right or wrong.

4. There is a famous case of corporate irresponsibility having to do with the design of the gas tank of the Ford Pinto in the early 1970's. Research this case, concentrating on the role of the Ford engineers. Does the engineer's ethical responsibility to protect the public apply here, and should they have blown the whistle on this questionable design?

5. The Challenger Space Shuttle blew up in 1986, 73 seconds into its tenth mission, killing all seven crew members. Was this disaster primarily caused by bad engineering, bad management, political pressure placed on NASA managers, or lack of communication between the engineers and NASA management? Who do you think was ultimately at fault? What can an engineer take away from this story?

---

[19] www.umich.edu/~thecore/doc/Friedman.pdf

Chapter Five
The Employment Contract

Part One: To Negotiate or Not

If one of your job interviews upon graduation leads to an offer of employment, congratulations. Your future supervisor or the human resources person you've been talking to will offer you a salary. Is it fair? Could you get more? If your name were Donald J. Trump, you know what you'd do. But, it's most likely not. So what exactly should you do?

You will be given some time to decide, so before you agree to anything, it would be a good idea to do as much research as you can as to the current distribution of salaries being offered to engineering graduates in your discipline, in the city where your job is located, at companies of the same general size, and any other relevant comparable characteristics. You will likely be able to find either the median salary, or a range of comparable offers, say from the 25th to the 75th percentile. If that range is small, say a few thousand dollars, and your offer is in that range, there is little that may be gained from negotiating. After all, an increase of $1,000 per year is equivalent to one latte per day. If that seems worthwhile to you, there is little harm in asking. You'll either get a yes or a no. If the range is large, and your offer seems to be on the low end, ask why. You are entitled to an answer. Be polite and respectful, always.

The fact of the matter is, you don't have too much negotiating leverage as a recent graduate. You can gain some strength in the process by having another job offer, better grades, a relevant capstone project, courses that prepare you as directly as possible for the job being offered, co-op or intern experiences, and excellent reference letters. Use them in your argument. But in the end, the company has the upper hand in this process. You can't get a really bad deal because it's a free market. The company needs an employee, and if you and everyone else offered this job decide that the offer is below par and turn it down, the company has no alternative but to offer a more competitive wage.

Don't neglect to ask for moving expenses if your job is in a different city than where you are living. Many companies will provide that. Find out as much as you can about benefits like health insurance, vacation policies, retirement plans (yes, you will want to retire some day), etc. These features of your offer are fixed and non-negotiable, since they will be uniform for all employees. Salary on the other hand is generally an individual matter.

During your discussions, listen very carefully for any statements involving the words "at will", or regarding the company's intentions to guarantee that you can work for, say a year, during which you will be trained and will not be fired. These are important stipulations that have legal consequences. An "at will" employee can be fired at any time, with certain limitations. If you are given a verbal guarantee of continuing employment, you should ask that the guarantee be put in writing for your protection.

Part Two: The Written Contract

You may be offered a written contract to sign. These documents are generally composed by lawyers for the benefit of the company, and you are strongly advised to have your own attorney go over it with you. Legal documents contain peculiar and confusing language to the uninitiated, yet these strange phrases have specific legal meanings that you must understand and agree to before you sign the document. Once you sign it, you are legally committed to its provisions. The best advice to follow with any contract is: if an attorney wrote it, have one read it. The cost will be nominal, and it could save you a great deal in the long run.

The "At Will" Employee

Take a look at the following excerpt of a sample contract[20] for an "at will" employee.

> This Employment Agreement is made effective for all purposes and in all respects as of this ____ day of _____, 2004, by and between _____, (hereinafter known as "Employer") and _____ (hereinafter known as "Employee") who shall collectively be known herein as "the Parties".

---

[20] www.scribd.com/doc/36757883/Sample-Employment-Contract

RECITALS:

WHEREAS, Employer is engaged in the business of _____;

WHEREAS, Employer wishes to employ Employee and Employee wishes to accept such employment on the terms and under the conditions recited below; The premises having been considered and with acknowledgment of the mutual promises and of other good and valuable consideration herein contained, the Parties, intending to be legally bound, hereby agree as follows:

A. Capacity of Employment. The duties to be performed by Employee for Employer are generally described as follows: design systems as directed.

B. Term of Employment—At Will Employee. Employer shall employ Employee in the capacity set forth above commencing on __/__/____ (or such other date as the Parties may agree to) and continuing, with no fixed termination date, until either Party shall give proper notice of termination of this employment agreement to the other.

No fixed contract period. There shall be no fixed date for termination of this employment agreement and it shall continue indefinitely until either Party gives proper notice to the other as required in this paragraph. Furthermore, Employee specifically waives any rights he or she may or may not have under state law (such as the Model Employment Termination Act or like legislation) requiring that any and all termination of employment be "for good cause". This is an "at will" employment arrangement and, as such, no cause is required by either party for termination hereof.

Notice Period. Any Party wishing to give notice of termination of this agreement, or of an intention not to renew at the end of a contract period, shall give the other Party ten days advance notice. The notice period does not commence until actually received by the other Party. Should state or federal law require a longer notice period, the longer notice period so required under the law shall be applicable to this contract.

C. Termination for cause. Employer may terminate this employment agreement at any time "for cause", the grounds for which are defined below. In the case of termination for cause, Employer shall have no obligation to Employee for salary, bonus, or other compensation or any other form of benefits under this agreement except for: (a) compensation earned prior to the effective date of termination, (b) vested benefits Employee has accrued under any retirement or deferred compensation plan sponsored by Employer, or (c) other benefits mandated under state or federal law for departed employees (such as COBRA health benefits). Also, in the case of termination for cause, Employer shall reimburse Employee for all appropriately documented expenses incurred by Employee before the termination date that are otherwise reimbursable to Employee under this contract. The "notice period" and "notice method", if any, contained in paragraph B above do **not** apply to termination for cause. Employer must give actual notice to Employee of termination for cause but may deliver said notice by any manner, either orally or in writing. Employer may make termination for cause effective immediately. Should state or federal law require a notice period, the notice period so required under the law shall be applicable to this contract. **This is an "at will" employment contract** wherein no cause is required for termination. This paragraph concerning "for cause" termination, if triggered through commission of the below acts by the Employee, merely allows the Employer to terminate without complying with the notice provisions contained in the preceding paragraph.

Grounds For "Cause" Termination. Commission of any of the following acts by Employee constitute grounds for the Employer to terminate Employee "for cause" under this paragraph:
1. Employee is charged with a felony crime;
2. Employee commits a crime of moral turpitude such as an act of fraud or other crime involving dishonesty;
3. Employee uses illegal drugs;
4. Employee fails to perform his or her duties in a competent manner;
5. Employee violates his or her duties of confidentiality and/or non–competition under this agreement;
6. Employee accepts an offer for future employment with a competitor of employer;
7. Employee fails to comply with directives from superiors, the company board of directors or managing officers, or written company policies;
8. Employee commits any act or acts that harm the Company's reputation, standing, or credibility within the community(ies) it operates or with its customers or suppliers;
9. Employee fails to perform the duties assigned to him or her for any reason.

The most important point to understand about this contract excerpt is the definition and implications of an "at will" employee. This is stated succinctly in paragraph B:

> *Employer shall employ Employee ... with no fixed termination date, until either Party shall give proper notice of termination of this employment agreement to the other... There shall be no fixed date for termination of this employment agreement and it shall continue indefinitely until either Party gives proper notice to the other as required in this paragraph. Furthermore, Employee specifically waives any rights he or she may or may not have under state law (such as the Model Employment Termination Act or like legislation) requiring that any and all termination of employment be "for good cause". This is an "at will" employment arrangement and, as such, no cause is required by either party for termination hereof.*

And further, the requirements for "notice" is given:

Any Party wishing to give notice of termination of this agreement, or of an intention not to renew at the end of a contract period, shall give the other Party ten days advance notice.

The "at will" employee is the most common arrangement for employment in our society. Most employees never read a contract such as this one. You're hired, with the understanding that you can leave whenever you want, and that your boss can fire you whenever, and for whatever reason. Nowadays, as more lawyers get into every facet of our lives, companies are using these employment contracts more often, to protect themselves from employees that may claim that they were told that they would *not* be fired except if they *did something wrong.* In this contract, such an action is called *termination for cause,* and the list of employee situations considered to be cause enough to fire someone is given in paragraph C, above. If fired *for cause,* no notice need be given. The employer can walk up to you and say, "leave right now." But, in fact, as you can see, the employer needs no cause at all to fire an "at will" employee. As stated in this contract, the employer need only give the employee ten days' notice, and need never explain why.

Note that some of the grounds for termination for cause are subject to "interpretation." What your employer may believe to be your failure to perform your duties *in a competent manner* may not comport with your feelings on the matter. Be that as it may, your employer can assert management prerogative and expel you from the premises! Your only recourse is to sue, but what good would that be? Paying a lawyer to gain perhaps ten more days of employment doesn't make much sense. On the other hand, *some* states have laws that restrict an employer's right to fire an at-will employee based on what is called a *public policy exception.* Thus, if the state has laws prohibiting certain forms of discrimination, for example, and it can be proven that the employer fired you as an act of discrimination prohibited by the law, then you could conceivably recover lost pay or other benefits. At will employees have brought suits against their employers for all kinds of reasons, charging intentional infliction of emotional distress, wrongful transfer or demotion, etc. These are all very unfortunate situations, and lawsuits of this nature can exact great financial and emotional tolls.

The Fixed Term Contract

From the employee's point of view, there is one advantage to being "at will." There is no obligation for the employee to remain at the job if a better one turns up somewhere else. If the employee had agreed to a fixed period of employment, it is possible that there could be some penalties for leaving before that period has expired. At least, a negotiation between the employee and employer would be necessary. The following contract is of that type, and offers a senior management position to an individual in an engineering/manufacturing company. Much more of this contract is reproduced below, because there are several issues that are very important to understand.

EMPLOYMENT AGREEMENT

Agreement made this 01st day of August, 1999 between AMG, Inc., a Nevada corporation (the "Company") and Mr. X, ("Employee").

WITNESSETH:

WHEREAS, the parties acknowledge that Employee has abilities and expertise that are unique and valuable to the Company; and

WHEREAS, in view of such abilities and expertise, the Company desire to retain Employee as Senior Vice President/General Manager; and

WHEREAS, the Company and Employee have determined that such engagement of Employee be subject to a mutually acceptable written agreement;

NOW THEREFORE, in consideration of the mutual agreements contained herein and intending to be legally bound, the parties hereto agree as follows:

1. SERVICES

(a) The Company hereby employs Employee and Employee hereby accepts such employment on the terms and conditions set forth herein. In this regard, Employee shall perform and discharge well and faithfully the duties and responsibilities that are commensurate with his position.

(b) Employee is not and shall not be engaged directly or indirectly in any other business activity, or previously have contracted to perform such activity at a future date which would prevent the performance of the obligations hereunder or involve activities which would result in a breach of any provision of this Agreement.

2. TERM

(a) The term of this Agreement shall begin on the date hereof and shall cease and terminate upon the earliest of (i) the close of business on the 1st day of August, 2001, (ii) the death of Employee; (iii) termination by the Company, at its option, for "cause" as defined in subdivision (b) of this Section 2; or (iv) termination by mutual agreement between the parties.

(b) As used in this Section, "cause" shall mean and be limited to gross negligence or willful misconduct of Employee in the performance of his duties, or conviction of a felony or a crime involving moral turpitude.

(c) In the event of a permanent disability, the contract will remain in effect until the start of long-term disability insurance coverage (3 months).

3. COMPENSATION

(a) The Company shall pay to Employee a base salary of $135,000 per year, payable in weekly installments.

(b) During the term of his employment, Employee shall be entitled to participate in employee benefit plans or programs of the Company, if any, to the extent his position, tenure, salary, age, health and other qualifications makes him eligible to participate, subject to the rules and regulations applicable thereto, which plans or programs will include, without limitation, health insurance benefits, performance-based options, an appropriate automobile allowance, and bonus programs, consistent with the reasonable past practices of the Company.

(c) The Company reserves the right to increase the compensation of the Employee, specified in this Instrument, at any time or times hereafter and no such increase or adjustment shall operate as a cancellation of this Agreement, but merely as an amendment to Section 3, and all the other terms, provision, and conditions of this Agreement shall continue in force and effect as herein provided.

(d) The Company will review this contract for consideration of a one (1) year extension when contract is 60 days from expiration.

4. EXPENSES

The Company will reimburse Employee for direct out-of-pocket expenses properly incurred by him in his performance of this Agreement and provided that a written accounting is made to the Company by Employee.

5. CONFIDENTIALITY AND NON-COMPETITION

(5.1) Employee acknowledges that as a consequence of his relationship with the Company, he has been and will continue to be given access to confidential information which may include the following types information: financial statements and related financial information with respect to the Company, trade secrets, computer programs, certain methods of operation, procedures, improvements, systems, customer lists, supplier lists and specifications, and other private and confidential materials concerning the Company's business (collectively, "Confidential Information"). Employee agrees that he shall maintain any Confidential Information in strictest confidence and shall not disclose any Confidential information to third parties during the terms of this agreement and after the termination hereof, however such termination shall occur, unless previously approved by the President or Chairman of AMG in writing.

Notwithstanding the foregoing, nothing herein shall be construed as prohibiting Employee from disclosing any Confidential Information

(a) which, at the time of disclosure, Employee can demonstrate either was in the public domain and generally available to the public or thereafter became a part of the public domain and generally available to the public by publication or otherwise through no act of Employee;

(b) which Employee can establish was independently developed by a third party who developed it without the use of the Confidential Information and who did not acquire it directly or indirectly from Employee under an obligation of confidence;

(c) which Employee can show was received by him after the termination of this Agreement from a third party who did not acquire it directly or indirectly from the Company under an obligation of confidence; or

(d) to the extent that Employee can reasonably demonstrate such disclosure is required by law or in any legal proceeding, governmental investigation, or other similar proceeding.

(5.2) Employee covenants and agrees that, in order to protect the company's interest in its business, operations and assets during the term of this Agreement and for a period of one (1) year following the termination of this Agreement, however the same shall occur, he will not, without prior written consent of the Company, directly or indirectly:

(a) engage anywhere in the United States, whether by virtue of stock ownership, management responsibilities or otherwise, in companies, business, organizations and/or ventures which are directly or indirectly competitive with the business of the Company as presently conducted or contemplated (the "Business"); or

(b)   become interested, directly or indirectly, whether as principal, owner, stockholder, partner, agent, officer, director, employee, salesman, joint venture, consultant, advisor, independent contractor or otherwise, in any person, firm, partnership, association, venture, corporation or entity engaging anywhere in the United State in the Business or directly or indirectly in competition with the Company.

6. INVENTIONS

(a) Employee hereby sells, transfers and assigns to the Company, or to any person or entity designated by the Company, all of the entire right, title and interest of Employee in and to all inventions, ideas, disclosures and improvements, whether patented or unpatented, and copyrightable materials, made or conceived by Employee, solely or jointly, or in whole or in part, during or before the term hereof which (i) relate to methods, apparatus, designs, products, processes or devices sold, leased, used or under construction or development by the Company, or (ii) otherwise relate, pertain or are useful to the business, functions or operations of the Company as presently conducted or to be conducted by the Company.

(b)   Employee shall communicate promptly and disclose to the Company, in such form as the Company requested, all information, details and data pertaining to the aforementioned inventions, ideas, disclosures and improvements; and whether during the term hereof or thereafter, Employee shall execute and deliver to the company such formal transfers and assignments and such other papers and documents as may be required of the Employee to permit the company or any person or entity designated by the Company to file and prosecute the patent applications and, as to copyrightable material, to obtain copyright thereon. Any invention by Employee within one year following the termination of this Agreement shall be deemed to fall within the provisions of this paragraph unless proved by Employee to have been first conceived and made following such termination.

7. NO WAIVER

The failure of any party to insist upon the strict performance of any of the terms, conditions or provisions of this Agreement shall not be construed as a waiver of relinquishment of future compliance therewith, and said terms, conditions and provisions shall remain in full force and effect. No interpretation, changes, modifications, terminations or waivers of any of the provisions of this Agreement shall be binding upon the Company or Employee unless in writing and signed by the person to be bound.

8. RIGHTS, OBLIGATIONS AND ASSIGNMENT

The rights and obligations of the Company under this Agreement shall inure to the benefit of, and shall be binding upon, its successors and assigns. The duties of Employee to any such successor entity shall not be greater than duties performed for the Company prior to such succession. Employee is prohibited from making any assignment of this Agreement.

9. ENTIRE AGREEMENT

This Agreement and the exhibits hereto embody the entire understanding between the parties hereto pertaining to the subject matter hereto and supersedes all prior agreements and understanding of the parties in connection therewith.

12. APPLICABLE LAW

This Agreement shall be enforced and construed in accordance with the laws of the State of California.

13. DISPUTES

In the event any party brings legal proceedings to resolve a dispute hereunder, the prevailing party shall have the right to recover reasonable attorneys' fees and costs from the other. The term "legal proceedings" shall include appeals from the lower court judgment.

14. PAYMENT ON TERMINATION

If the Company terminates this Agreement other than for cause as defined in Section 2(b) of this Agreement, it shall pay Employee an amount equal to the amount set forth in Section 3(a) as an annual base salary divided by twelve and multiplied by the number of months remaining until the 1st day of August, 2001.

So, we see that the contract begins on the first day of August, 1999 (first line), and ends two years later (paragraph 2a). The employee is to be paid $135,000 per year (paragraph 3a). The contract terminates if the employee dies, or for "cause" as defined in 2b, or by *mutual agreement between the parties*. Thus, if the employee wants to leave before Aug. 2001, but the company doesn't agree, there will be a conflict. Paragraph 13 indicates how disputes will be handled. Only "legal proceedings" are contemplated, i.e., law suits, and the loser has to pay the costs of the winner. That's a very strong factor to dissuade the use of the courts, since such actions are extremely expensive. (A better alternative might be to settle disputes by *binding arbitration*, where an arbitrator is selected, agreeable to both sides, and the arbitrator's decision is final and cannot be appealed.) On the other hand, the employer can terminate the contract without cause, if it wants to. Paragraph 14 says that the employer can terminate the employee by merely paying the rest of the compensation due through to the end of the contract. So, you see the employee has some significant economic protection, and the term of the contract is not unduly long, and can be extended if mutually agreed.

Confidentiality Clause

Two very significant parts of this agreement are spelled out in paragraphs 5 and 6. Paragraph 5 deals with two issues, *confidentiality* and *non-competition*. The confidentiality clause is reminiscent of the situation faced by the ancient Pharaohs of Egypt. They were traditionally buried with all their enormous wealth of gold and jewels in an inner chamber of a pyramid that was built for that specific purpose. Of course, these tombs were very attractive to thieves once the Pharaoh was buried. In order to secure his tomb from these grave robbers, a Pharaoh made sure that no one who knew how the pyramid was constructed would ever reveal its secrets. This was simply accomplished by slaughtering the designers and all the workers who constructed the pyramid. Perfect confidentiality was assured.

Fortunately, we have a more restrained approach to confidentiality issues these days. The confidentiality clause (5.1) in the example contract restricts the employee from disclosing company-private, confidential information to anyone outside the company (*a third party*) during the term of the contract and indefinitely thereafter. This restriction is lifted (a) in case the information had already been disclosed publicly by someone else, or (b) it was "developed", that is independently thought up or invented by the third party or through an even more complicated route (c), or (d) the disclosure is required by law, which could occur if the company was being investigated by the government for a suspected illegal act. Such confidential information includes the company's financial information, trade secrets, computer programs, certain methods of operation, procedures, improvements, systems, customer lists, supplier lists and specifications. Confidentiality clauses are found in every employee contract in which the employee may have access to this information. As an engineer, you will have access to confidential information, so be prepared to agree to terms similar to these, throughout your career. Not every confidentiality clause will require you to keep the secrets indefinitely. More often, there will be a time limit of some number of years, after which the company feels secure that the information would be outdated or useless to its competitors.

The Non-Compete Clause

The second part of paragraph 5 concerns non-competition. The concern here is that the employee, after leaving the company, may want to work for another company that is a competitor. This non-competition clause attempts to prevent the ex-employee from transmitting information learned at the former company that may be advantageous to the new employer, even if that information is not confidential to the prior employer. The clause also seeks to prevent the ex-employee himself from competing directly or indirectly with the former company. The extent of the restrictions placed on the ex-employee by these types of clauses varies from contract to contract. A non-compete clause may restrict the ex-employee from working for a competitor only within 50 miles of the former company, or only within the same state, or anywhere in the country. The restriction may last only for a few months or for years. It also may be limited by types of products or market segments. In this particular contract, the competitors are defined as nation-wide (5.2 a), and the time limit is one year (5.2). There are two difficulties with this clause as stated here. First, the clause defines the "business" for which the restrictions apply as "the business of the Company as presently conducted or contemplated." The ex-employee may not know what business opportunities are being "contemplated" by the board of directors of the former company. This restriction is not transparent enough and can lead to disputes. In addition, if this clause were part of a contract with a huge multinational corporation with many different business interests, the ex-employee could be prevented from working in many industries. Secondly, the clause prevents the ex-employee from owning stock in a competing company, as defined by the broad definition of the company's business. Many individuals own shares in mutual funds that invest in hundreds of companies, and the individual shareholder has no control or prior knowledge of which companies the fund may invest in. Surely it is possible that the ex-employee may wind up owning shares of a competitor. This is another potential source of conflict.

It is not uncommon for ex-employees to sue their former companies on this issue of non-competition. From the employees' point of view, the non-compete clause could put them out of work for the period of time specified in the contract. If ex-employees have very specialized skills, and can only work in particular product or market segments, then the non-compete clause will shut them out of the employment market. These suits have resulted in limitations to the extent of the restrictions that are permitted. Since contract law is under the jurisdiction or each state, the legal limitations vary from state to state. Most states permit non-compete clauses to be enforced if they are "reasonable" in geographic extent and time limit imposed, and can be shown to be necessary to protect the former employer. In California, however, non-compete restrictions are illegal, except in contracts with major stakeholders, usually the founders of the company. Even though the laws of the state in which the contract will be enforced (see paragraph 12) may prohibit features of the non-compete clause, employers may still retain the unenforceable language as a psychological deterrent to the ex-employee. You can see the value of having a competent attorney read such a contract before you sign it. The lawyer can point out to you if the non-compete clause is in accord with the laws of the state, and suggest that you insist on modifications to bring the wording into compliance up front, if necessary!

Because engineers are so mobile in our society, you will likely work for several employers over the course of your career. The non-compete issue will surface again and again. It is also not true that simply because your job is in California, you will not have to worry about the non-compete problem. Many companies locate their corporate headquarters in states other than where their employees may work. This is done in order to benefit from the laws of the states that favor employers over employees! Some states have laws that are quite conservative, and reflect societal norms of a century ago. So, it is essential that you check out the paragraph that identifies which state's law applies to the contract (such as paragraph 12), and find a lawyer who is familiar with the laws of that state, and of the state in which you would be working, to give you guidance.

Inventions

Inventions are the lifeblood of technology companies. You may not believe that you could actually invent something, but engineers come up with innovative ideas all the time, and your ideas may be winners. As a general principle, anything of value created by employees as part of the job belongs to the employer, because the employees are being paid for their labor. This is the basis for the invention clause (paragraph 13) in the above contract. This invention clause states generally, but in more precise legal terms, that employees agree to give to the company all rights to their inventions and other valuable works that are related to the business interests of the company. These business interests include *(i)* ... *methods, apparatus, designs, products, processes or devices sold, leased, used or under construction or development by the Company, or (ii) otherwise relate, pertain or are useful to the business, functions or operations of the Company as presently conducted or to be conducted by the Company* (6a). The inventions may be conceived *during or before the term hereof*, or *within one year following the termination of this Agreement* (6b), unless the employee can prove that the initial idea originated after leaving the company.

Several things are troubling about this clause. First, if the invention was conceived *before* the employee started working at the company, why should the employee give up rights to it? Secondly, there is this problem again of the activities that the company may decide to get into in the future. Why couldn't a cagey company president, upon hearing of an employee's invention that has nothing to do with the present activities of the company, start thinking about getting into a business related to that new idea, thereby providing a basis for taking the employee's invention away? A lawyer could give you an opinion as to whether or not that were permissible, but the wording of this invention clause seems to make that scenario possible.

Although not stated in this particular invention clause, an employee tinkering at home with an idea that has nothing to do with the company, would be wise to assiduously avoid using any materials, computers, pens, pencils, pads of paper... anything... that is rightfully the property of the company. Did you take a pad of paper home to work on a company problem? That would normally be fine, but don't use it to write your notes about your new idea! The company might have a right to claim ownership because you used its property in developing your invention!

Essay Questions

1) Setting aside the rather generous salary in the contract offered by AMG, and the bonus, and the automobile allowance (nice perks!), would you have any concerns about signing this agreement? Are there any parts of it that you don't understand?

2) Investigate the positions taken by any of the engineering societies with respect to invention or non-compete clauses in employment contracts. What actions are being taken to improve the laws of the states on behalf of engineering employees?

3) Look up Section 2870 of the California Labor Code and consider the following:

   How does paragraph (a)(1) of the statute apply if, for example, you are a programmer developing computer games for a company, and also programming your own game project at home on your own computer? Does it matter that your game was not in the company's development plans?

4) Research and discuss the "public policy exception" to employment "at will."

Chapter Six
Patents

If GM had kept up with technology like the computer industry has,
we would all be driving $25 cars that got 1000 MPG   - Bill Gates

To invent, you need a good imagination and a pile of junk
- Thomas Alva Edison

Part One: What is a Patent?

US Patents are issued by the federal government in accordance
with the Constitution of the United States, which states: *"The Congress
shall have power to... promote the progress of science and useful arts, by
securing for limited times to authors and inventors the exclusive right to their
respective writings and discoveries."* When the US Patent and Trademark
Office issues a patent to an inventor, that inventor is given *"the right to
exclude others from making, using, offering for sale, or selling"* the invention
in the United States or importing the invention into the United States.
What is granted is *not* the right to make, use, offer for sale, sell or
import, but the right to *exclude other*s from making, using, offering for
sale, selling or importing the invention. This is a very important
distinction, since in our society, everyone already *has* the right to
conduct legal business affairs. A patent *limits* these rights, temporarily,
to the patent owner. Thus, a patent could be of great commercial value,
since it creates a time-limited monopoly, currently 20 years, and as it is
owned by the inventor (or someone to whom the patent is assigned,
including possibly a fictitious "person" such as a corporation), it is very
much like real property, and can be bought and sold, leased (licensed)
to another party, or traded in any manner in which any other property
may be traded. This type of property is correctly referred to as
intellectual property, or *IP.*

The rules governing patents are established by federal law. A
patent may be obtained by anyone, whether a citizen of the US or not,
who "invents or discovers any new and useful process, machine,
manufacture, or composition of matter, or any new and useful
improvement thereof." These categories are meant to be interpreted
very widely, so a "process" can be anything from a recipe and
procedure for baking bread to a software algorithm. In fact, these
categories taken together are meant to include practically everything

that can be made by man and the processes for making them. Only a few exclusions exist, such as processes for making an atomic bomb! Also, one cannot patent laws of nature, physical phenomena, or abstract ideas.

The subject matter of a patent must be "useful", which implies that the invention or discovery can be realized, and made to work or perform as intended. In order to prove this in the past, the inventor was required to provide a miniature model of the invention to the patent office that showed how the invention worked. Fortunately, this is no longer required! These models, many of them works of art in themselves, were sold by the patent office in 1925, and are now owned by museums and collectors. The model shown here is a miniature "Machine for Cutting Lozenges," dating from 1871[21].

[21] Courtesy of Rothchild Patent Model Collection

Instead of a working miniature model, the law now requires that the inventor provide a complete description of the subject matter, with enough detail so that a person of "ordinary skill in the art" of the invention can make and use the invention without "undue experimentation". This person of *ordinary skill in the art* is a fictional individual having normal skills and knowledge in a particular technical field, without being a genius. These rather vague definitions have lead to much argument and legal conflicts, as you might imagine.

In addition to being "useful", an invention must be "new". US law therefore requires that the invention was not described in a printed document anywhere in the world, or known or used by others in the US, prior to the date that the invention was made. In addition, the patent application must be made within one year of the appearance of a printed description or use of the invention in the US. The rules in other countries are different, so if you want to patent your invention in Europe as well as the US, for example, you will need to meet their rules as well.

The requirement that an invention be previously unknown leads to another concept, that of "obviousness". A person cannot obtain a patent by making a modification to an existing invention, or by combining any number of existing inventions in a manner that a person of ordinary skill in the art would think is *obvious*. So now there are *two* questions that can lead to potential conflict, which may arise not only during the process of convincing a patent examiner to allow the patent to issue, but also if someone is sued for patent *infringement*[22] — those two contentious questions are

- ❖ Is the invention non-obvious in light of all the *prior art*, that is, all the existing inventions that are known?

- ❖ Since the obviousness question depends on the opinion of a fictitious person *with ordinary skill in the art*, how do we know what that person would think?

These questions come up repeatedly in patent litigation cases, and huge amounts of money can hang in the balance. The cases are heard in federal court, and may be decided by a jury made up of individuals having absolutely no knowledge of the scientific underpinnings of the invention. Imagine the problems faced by the

---

[22] In a suit for patent infringement, the defendant is accused of violating the monopoly granted the patent holder.

attorneys in these cases, trying to advance the point of view favorable to their respective clients by educating an average juror of the obviousness or non-obviousness of a tweak to a computer algorithm, a new microchip design, or a modification to a chemical process to produce a new drug. And when two "experts" are called to testify as to what an individual having ordinary skill in the art would think, and they don't agree, how would a juror know who's right? Perhaps that is why nine out of ten such cases are settled, and never go to trial.

You might have thought that once the US Patent and Trademark Office issues a patent, the patent is secure. That is not the case. A patent can be declared invalid by court action. For example, in a patent infringement action, a judge can rule that the evidence presented supports the finding that the invention was obvious, or invalid for other reasons, and the patent would be lost. Other legal challenges can also be raised. For example, anyone may request re-examination of a patent by the patent office, and bring new evidence of prior art to the attention of the patent office that might not have been available when the patent was first issued. In such an action, the patent office itself may either reaffirm the patent or nullify it.

Part Two: Patents at Work

<u>Helping Your Company Obtain a Patent</u>

Engineers work on innovative products and processes all the time. In case your own work leads to an invention that is potentially patentable, it is essential that you follow your company's policies with respect to documenting your work, especially when you think of new useful ideas. Companies generally require that their engineers working on potentially patentable products or processes keep a bound notebook, and write down the details of any new and useful ideas, sign and date the entry, and have a colleague who was not involved in the development of the idea sign the page in your notebook, with a date and the notation that the entry was read and understood. These notebook entries can sometimes become critical evidence if a competing firm claims a similar invention. In the US, the patent goes to the first to invent and reduce an invention to practice, that is, work out all the details, and do the necessary testing to prove that the invention works. All these steps should be recorded in your notebook.

Your company may decide to try to get a patent, or not. Applying for a patent is a time-consuming and expensive activity, so your management will weigh the potential benefits with the costs. If the company decides to go for it, you will be asked to help the patent attorney write the description of the patent, help find the relevant prior art, and sign a document giving up your rights to the invention and assigning them to your company. If you signed an employment contract, you probably agreed to help your company acquire patents in just this way. See for example paragraph 6(b) in the fixed term contract presented in Chapter 5.

Helping Your Company Avoid Infringement

If you are working in a highly competitive field, it is likely that there are thousands of patents that have been issued, or that are in the patent pipeline, relating to the technology you are working on. For example, if you are working on a product that includes a small electronic display, it is likely to be an LCD (liquid crystal display). There are more than 5,500 US patents still in force that reserve rights to various aspects of that technology. Almost 1,000 deal with the features and applications of touch screens. It is important that you maintain an awareness of the patent landscape in your area of specialization. You should know who your competitors are, if possible. You should search the patent office website[23] for new patents related to your field. First of all, it is a great source of ideas, many times even more descriptive and readable than journal articles. This can point you in new directions that you may not have thought about before. Be careful to record in your notebook that your new direction was based on someone else's invention! But you would provide a major service to your company if you come across a patent that is so close to what your company is planning to do, that your product may infringe that patent. You must discuss this with your supervisor. Preventing your company from spending a great deal of money to develop a product only to find that someone else invented it earlier would be a very important contribution. It is notoriously difficult to know for sure if your product infringes earlier patents, for the reasons suggested above, relating to obviousness. Minute differences may be deciding factors. It is essential that an experienced IP attorney be consulted. But your management would have an obligation to investigate the issue, and either decide to drop the product, modify it so greatly using your company's own

---

[23] http://patft.uspto.gov/

innovative ideas that it no longer infringes, or try to get the permission of the holder of the earlier patent to use the prior invention. Most companies *license* patents between each other all the time. Such licenses permit companies to profit from their patents even if they never had plans to use the idea themselves in a product.

The Value of IP

Large companies that support a substantial research effort may apply for thousands of patents each year. Since 1992, IBM has led the list of corporations being granted the largest number of patents each year. The top ten list for 2009 is shown below:

1	IBM	4,914		6	Toshiba	1,696
2	Samsung	3,611		7	Sony	1,680
3	Microsoft	2,906		8	Intel	1,537
4	Canon	2,206		9	Seiko Epson	1,330
5	Panasonic	1,829		10	HP	1,273

For IBM, that's an astonishing 19 granted patents per work day! According to IBM, about one-third of its patents are used in IBM products, and over 30,000 IBM patents are available for licensing to other companies. This licensing activity has been reported to provide about $1 billion each year to the company. Microsoft's licensing income has been estimated to be three times larger! Microsoft's chief IP officer said that patents are treated not as a profit center but "as a currency that you use to trade to another company" for *its* patents.

At the other end of the corporate spectrum from these giants are companies for which patents may be relatively even *more* valuable. These are companies with few employees, net operating losses, existing precariously on loans or investments for which their potentially worthless stock has been promised in return. What are these companies, and why would anyone invest in such enterprises? These are *high tech start-ups*, companies with a bold idea for a new product. An important attraction for venture capitalists to invest in these risky affairs is the protection afforded by the IP these companies own. In fact, often the only assets a start-up has may be its patents. Will those patents be commercially valuable? Might they be overturned? The risks are great, as are the potential rewards.

Essay Questions

1) Find a patent of interest in your intended area of specialization. You may use a Boolean search engine on the website of the US Patent and Trademark Office, http://patft.uspto.gov/. Describe the several sections of the patent, and analyze and comment on the linguistic structure of the claims.

2) What is a "patent pool" and how does it work? What problem might it solve?

3) What is a "patent troll"? Find an example of an individual or company that has been labeled as such and investigate the charge.

4) Find and research a recent patent infringement case that has been discussed on the web. Look for one that was decided on the basis of "obviousness." What were the issues?

5) In 2007, the Supreme Court ruled on a case called, "KSR International Co. v. Teleflex Inc." This ruling has been called the Court's furthest-reaching patent ruling in decades. What was the case about, and what effect might the decision have? Do you agree with the Court's findings?

Chapter Seven
Outsourcing and The Global Marketplace

Every morning in Africa, a gazelle wakes up. It knows it must run faster than the fastest lion or it will be killed. Every morning a lion wakes up. It knows it must outrun the slowest gazelle or it will starve to death. It doesn't matter whether you are a lion or a gazelle... when the sun comes up, you'd better be running. – African Saying

The only one who can guarantee your job is a healthy and satisfied customer.
– Harry C. Stonecipher

Part One: The Inexorable Attraction(?) of Outsourcing

We are witnessing a rapid expansion in the technical capabilities of many countries around the world. It had been reported that China, for example, graduated almost nine times the number of engineers than did the US in 2004, (600,000 *vs* 70,000). Both these numbers have been contradicted after further analysis, and the most recent reports suggest that the numbers of four-year college, BS-level engineers produced by China and by the US are roughly comparable, in spite of the fact that China's population is over four times larger. Whatever the numbers may be, the fact is that China, and progressively India as well, are graduating BS-level engineers in very large numbers.

Whereas Chinese companies fabricate and export a huge number and quantity of *products*, some of which may have been designed in the US, most of the outsourcing of *services*, like engineering work, is done in India. It is especially important to consider the competitive advantages that India's engineering force might provide to companies in the US. In the first place, due to India's colonial history, English is one of India's official languages, and is spoken by a large fraction of the educated class. Secondly, the salaries for engineers are very low by comparison to those in the US. For example, in 2010, a structural engineer working for a moderate size company in Mumbai, having 3 years of experience beyond the BS degree, would make the equivalent of about $15,000 per year. Software engineers with equivalent training may earn only half that. Electrical engineers with three years experience earn 400,000 to 500,000 rupees, between $8,000 and $10,000.

These salaries are at least a factor of four to six lower than US salaries. Thus, if you were the CEO of a US company, and you thought that you could get your engineering work done in India, what would *you* do? Not only is the direct cost of labor an incredible bargain, but you don't have to pay for employee medical insurance, social security taxes, retirement... It looks like a no-brainer.

But is it? There are two ways to implement an outsourcing effort. You could, for example, set up an Indian affiliate company. Lots of hassles there: buying land, building a facility, or leasing one; finding a really good manager with experience with the Indian system, and knowledge of your business; hiring staff; regulations to learn about; taxes to pay; fluctuations in the exchange rate, the list goes on and on... Or, you could contract with an outsourcing company[24] that has all the engineers on staff, in offices in India, ready to get to work. The result is no direct management hassles for you. The two largest Indian outsourcing service firms are Wipro Technologies and Infosys. But the largest outsourcing service organization of all, with 160,000 employees in India alone, is IBM![25] Of course, you have to pay a lot more than just the salaries of the engineers who will be working on your project. Included are the costs of infrastructure and management of the outsourcing company plus their profit. Many companies, large and small, have found that it is still significantly less expensive to outsource engineering work to India than to do the work in the US, in most cases.

The one huge problem that remains is making sure that the work can be done to your satisfaction. After several years of experience with outsourcing, there is a strong difference of opinion on that subject. Some companies swear by it, while other firms, having suffered unexpected setbacks or unanticipated costs, are convinced that outsourcing engineering work is not a good idea. Here are some of the pros and cons, from the corporate point of view:

---

[24] As of 2010, there were over 700 such companies advertising on the web.

[25] Data as of 2010. That year, IBM projected a 25% yearly growth of employees in India. Not all are engineers, of course.

Advantages of Outsourcing

- Access to professional, experienced personnel for limited periods of time, if necessary, to initiate and complete special projects for which your company doesn't have the required expertise

- Increased flexibility — take on new projects that you wouldn't have attempted to do before

- No need to invest in the latest technology, software or infrastructure, since your outsourcing partner will be doing that and sharing the costs among its many clients

- Cut your operating costs by perhaps 50%

Disadvantages of Outsourcing

- Potential loss of confidentiality — your outsource partner may not be able to control access to your company's proprietary IP as well as you would. IP is very valuable, and who knows the ethics of the people employed by your outsource service provider

- If your outsource provider goes bankrupt, you will have to scramble to recover the work product, and restart the effort — many months can be lost

- Outsourcing is detrimental to company morale — all employees will think that their jobs will be the next to go

- You lose control over the day-to-day engineering process, and you may suffer long periods without feedback from the project managers — are they on track? Are they on schedule? Can you believe their progress reports?

- What if you need to make a change in the statement of work? Does your outsourcing contract impose penalties for such changes? Does the contract need to be renegotiated?

This last point is especially troublesome. Often, in the initial phase of a project, the scope and details of the work that will need to be done is unknown. If you leave the scope of work vague, you have no realistic way to measure the "deliverables," or complain about lack of performance. If the scope of work is made too restrictive, you lose the flexibility in following the best route to a successful conclusion of

71

the project. Ironing out the details of an outsourcing contract will take a great deal of time and will in itself be a costly exercise.

The Boeing Company provides a well-known example of the perils of outsourcing large and complex projects. Ten years before the first test flight of the 787 Dreamliner, Boeing announced that component fabrication would be spread among companies all over the world. Here's a rundown of some of the major aircraft components (just those visible from the outside of the plane!) and their production origin:

Forward fuselage	Spirit AeroSystems	USA
Fuselage, wheel well	Kawasaki	Japan
Center/aft fuselage	Alenia/Vought	Italy/USA
Landing gear	Messier-Dowty	France
Passenger doors	Latecoere	France
Cargo/access doors	Saab	Sweden
Engines	GE	USA
Engines	Rolls-Royce	UK
Outer engine casing	Goodrich	USA
Engine pylons	Spirit AeroSystems	USA
Wing box	Mitsubishi	Japan
Center wing box	Fuji	Japan
Leading edge	Spirit AeroSystems	USA
Wingtips	Korean Air Lines	South Korea
Fixed trailing edge	Kawasaki	Japan
Movable trailing edge	Hawker de Haviland	Australia
Wing-to-body fairing	Boeing Winnipeg	Canada
Horizontal stabilizer	Alenia/Vought	Italy/USA
Vertical tail	Boeing Frederickson	USA

Companies in Italy, France, UK, Sweden, Japan, Australia, Canada and the US as well were to provide components that would all work together, and be assembled in Boeing's plant near Everett, WA. Note that these companies are not in the developing countries of the world where labor costs are low. These companies are top-notch industrial producers with great reputations, many with long years of prior experience as Boeing suppliers. Boeing chose to distribute the work internationally to enhance future sales in those countries. As the announced date of the first test flight neared, in spite of Boeing's very precisely-specified engineering requirements for these outsourced components, reports of production delays from many companies in the supply chain forced a two-year production postponement, and billions in lost sales. So, even a company as experienced with outsourcing as Boeing can fall victim to the complexities of managing such an enterprise.

Part Two: Effects of Outsourcing, at Home and Abroad

As a student engineer, looking at the job market and anticipating a fruitful career, you will undoubtedly be concerned about the outsourcing trend. Will engineering jobs in the US disappear?

Numbers are hard to come by. Although the more than 700 outsourcing firms offering services in India have in total hundreds of thousands of employees, only a small fraction of them will be engineers. There will be lots of accountants, lots of customer service people answering phone calls at phone banks, even radiologists interpreting X-rays for hospitals. The true number of engineering professionals working for outsourcing providers in India is not known. And even if it were, these engineers work on projects for companies throughout the world — Europe, Japan, and India itself. The fraction of time they spend on US contract engineering projects is unknown.

Trying a different tack, one can look at the unemployment rate of US engineers. Even during the recession of 2008-2009, while the general unemployment rate in the US rose to greater than 10%, annual unemployment rates for engineers as a group rose to about 5%, and then started to fall even as the general unemployment rate continued to rise. Prior to that recession, engineering unemployment rates hovered around 2%, in spite of the fact that outsourcing was increasing at that same time. The number of US engineers employed shows no downward trend that can be attributed to the increase in outsourcing. If there is such a trend, the effects are in the noise, overwhelmed by fluctuations more dependent on the business climate.

If you were inclined to be pessimistic about jobs, you could postulate some nasty long-term trends — corporations learn how to avoid the disadvantages of outsourcing engineering projects, and gain confidence in the quality of outsourcing service providers, etc. The fact is, the future could go either way.

In 2004, Harry Stonecipher, Boeing President and CEO, spoke[26] at an annual meeting of the Orange County Business Council, and presented a very well-reasoned case in support of outsourcing. His points are summarized below:

- ❖ Companies should concentrate on their core competencies and outsource what they cannot do as well.

- ❖ Outsourcing to foreign countries is a form of world trade. It increases the economic strength of our trading partners, and not only helps us to develop relationships that can lead to sales of our products there, but also helps foreign companies to create advanced products at lower cost that we import, resulting in a higher standard of living here.

- ❖ The US has had it so good for so long that it's unsettling to come to grips with the realization that we will have to compete for certain jobs with highly skilled and highly motivated workers in countries much less affluent than our own.

- ❖ The displacement of jobs and entire industries from region to region within the US has been going on for a long time, and these adjustments are painful. Outsourcing is an extension of that process to the international domain.

- ❖ "People need to learn, unlearn and relearn as technology and careers advance in the global marketplace." It is part of the job of a business leader to make that happen for your employees.

As the economic strength of China and India increase, it is inevitable that the cost of outsourcing to those countries will also increase. Witness the series of labor strikes against Honda in China in 2010. Salaries of those workers rose over 20%. Salaries in India are catching up to those in developed nations at a faster rate than in many other Asian countries, according to a recent report from London human resources firm ECA International. The trend to higher wages will continue. As wages go up for the lowest paid factory worker,

---

[26] Stonecipher's speech may be found at www.boeing.com/news/speeches/2004/stonecipher_040603.html.

74

wages will also rise for the engineer working for the outsource service provider. As a consequence, over time, there will be less incentive for projects to be outsourced on the basis of cost savings alone. The most important attractors will remain availability of expertise, quality of service, convenience and efficiency. There is no reason why US engineers cannot compete successfully on that playing field. Professionalism, and all its implications, is the key.

Part Three: Immigration Policies

Thomas L. Friedman, Op-Ed columnist at the New York Times, wrote an interesting piece[27] in 2007 after attending the commencement exercises at Rensselaer Polytechnic Institute, in which he chided the government because "there wasn't someone from the Immigration and Naturalization Service standing next to (Rensselaer's President) stapling green cards to the diplomas" of each of the foreign-born Ph.D.'s graduating that day. "I want them all to stay," he wrote, "become Americans and do their research and innovation here. If we can't educate enough of our own kids to compete at this level, we'd better make sure we can import someone else's, otherwise we will not maintain our standard of living."

Although immigration is a contentious political issue in our society, there should be little argument with Friedman's point of view. Ph.D. engineers comprise a very small fraction of the profession, many of them teaching at universities or doing advanced research at large corporations. As such they do not compete in any substantive way with BS- and MS-trained engineers. To the contrary, these elite engineers are job creators, and new technologies, new products, whole new industries have resulted from their efforts.

Much more controversial is a little-known immigration category called the H–1B visa. The H–1B is a non-immigrant visa designed to permit US companies to hire foreign workers in specialty occupations for a limited period of time. Except for the occupation of "fashion model" of "distinguished merit and ability," the foreign workers must have at least the equivalent of a bachelor's degree in a field of engineering, the sciences, medicine, education, or business, among

---

[27] "Laughing and Crying",
http://select.nytimes.com/2007/05/23/opinion/23friedman.html?_r=1

others. The visa holder may work in the US for three years, with a possible extension for another three. The unusual aspect of this visa is that a US employer must petition the Immigration Service to be a visa sponsor. If a visa is made available, the company may then find a foreign worker to hold that visa. If the job evaporates, of if the worker quits, the worker must leave the US immediately unless another job with another visa sponsor becomes available. Thus, the worker is in a precarious position, and many have argued that this position puts the foreign worker at such a disadvantage that complaints about unethical or illegal practices employed by the visa sponsor would be unlikely. Another feature of this program permits the visa holder to apply for a green card while on the H–1B visa. Often, the processing of a green card application will take so long that a decision will not be reached until after the foreign worker has returned home. Also, the spouse of an H–1B visa holder may not work in the US.

There are many regulations imposed by law to mitigate the effects of this program on the US job market. Thus, salaries offered to foreign workers are supposed to be no less than those offered to comparable US workers, and it is illegal to fire a US employee and then offer that job to a foreign worker. In addition, there is a cap on the number of H–1B visas that may be issued in each fiscal year. This cap has varied from a low of 65,000 to a high of 195,000. Many tens of thousands of foreign workers per year may find employment outside of this cap under various exceptions. Because of the large size of this program, enforcement of the regulations has been spotty.

The intent of the H–1B program was to increase the availability of highly skilled workers to offset a labor shortage claimed by corporate executives. Is there a true labor shortage of skilled engineers? Arguments fly on both sides of the issue. Corporate executives claim that they cannot find suitable US workers to fill open high-tech positions. Others point to the advantages that accrue to the employer if there is a *surplus* of such workers... wages will tend to decrease because of the principles of supply and demand, and the employer will have a larger pool of workers from which to choose.

Many companies sponsoring H–1B visas petition for a large number of visas. In 2006, the three US technology companies with the largest number of H–1B visas received were Microsoft (3,517 visas), Cognizant (2,226 visas) and IBM (1,130 visas). A darker side to these numbers is the fact that two companies received even more visas than Microsoft in 2006: the US affiliate of Infosys received 4,908 and the US affiliate of Wipro received 4,002. We recognize these companies as the largest outsourcing service providers in India. Critics maintain that Infosys and Wipro bring their Indian employees to the US on H–1B visas so that they can interact with US businesses, develop relationships with them, learn how these businesses operate, and then return to India in a few years after having attracted them as confirmed outsourcing clients. Should these visas be used to encourage this activity? Is it in the best interests of our country, our economy, or our professional labor force? These are controversial issues.

Part Four: Personal Strategies for Success

Whether or not Harry Stonecipher of Boeing makes convincing arguments to you, it is likely to be true that his prediction of the displacement of some engineering jobs will come to pass, and that the process will be painful to those whose jobs are affected. As engineering students, you have an opportunity to think about how to craft your career in order to maximize your chances of success. Students presented with this question have offered the following observations:

- Go for an advanced engineering degree or a double degree — students in India and China do not generally have the resources to stay in school for advanced degrees, and US companies need engineers with advanced training to design and innovate.

- Some engineering fields require on-site work, and cannot be outsourced — for example, engineers working for utilities companies, or those installing or maintaining large complex systems on customer's premises.

- Combine engineering with law (patent work) or with an MBA, with the intent to move into management. Engineering sales is also not easily outsourced because it requires face-to-face efforts with prospective customers.

- Master a second language. Better yet, get a job overseas, and develop an intimate understanding of another country, its language, culture, and political system.

- Seek engineering work in an industry supplying products or doing R&D for the military or for homeland security. These industries may require secret clearance (citizenship and a very clean record.)

❖ Start a company; become an entrepreneur! The boss doesn't get outsourced.

These are all great ideas — they are all bound to increase your desirability to an employer and/or bring more stability and predictability to your professional career.

In the event that you need to find a job, however, there is one more thing to keep in mind that will be very helpful. In spite of all the jobs listed online, a great many professionals will tell you that they found their best opportunities through tips from their professional associates, co-workers and former classmates — their professional *network*. Networking really works. As a student, your network is likely to be pretty sparse. At this early stage in your career, you can start to build your network by simply developing friendships with your classmates. If you're shy, strive to overcome that. Engineering students are often characterized as being less social than students in other fields. If you feel that you tend in that direction, make the effort to join some clubs or student organizations that will give you an opportunity to meet more people and become more at ease in social situations. Your classmates will disperse to all manner of engineering jobs, eventually, all over the country, if not the world — a terrific potential resource! By maintaining even a tenuous contact, such as a yearly holiday e-mail, an occasional note about what you're doing, where you're working, etc., you will be in a position to ask your old classmates if they know of a job opportunity for you if and when you need it. Cultivate your network. Add to it at every opportunity. Ask engineers you meet at trade shows to go to lunch with you. Find out what they do. Collect business cards. Keep in touch with those that are in your field or a related field. Join local chapters of your professional society, for sure. Talk to people. They'll remember you. Networking is mutually beneficial. Respond to requests from your network of contacts when they need *your* assistance. Think of it as a specialized information exchange and support mechanism — a source of highly relevant information you may need, supplied by other professionals in your discipline. People who have researched the art of networking claim that 80% of new job and business opportunities come from networking contacts! Don't neglect this extremely useful strategy.

Most students who plan for success hope that they will become excellent, top-notch engineers, and envision living up to that ideal by working very hard in school and maintaining their skills thereafter. Some students point to the expectation that as our society becomes ever more dependent on technology, engineering jobs will increase in spite of outsourcing, and that the advanced engineering skills of US-based companies will continue to attract work from other nations, a reverse outsourcing. Native-born engineering students are confident that their language skills will be an advantage to their employer, enabling better communication between engineer and management. And foreign students believe that their knowledge of their homelands will make them more valuable as well. All these observations, hopes, plans, and intentions are right on the money, literally and figuratively. It all goes back to being a *professional*. Make it so...

Essay Questions

1) Find out which of the professional engineering societies have issued policy statements or testified in Congress on the subject of the H-1B visa. Report and comment.

2) How has politics affected the H-1B visa laws?

3) Pick a large outsource service company and report on the varied engineering services that it can supply.

4) Find an article describing recent experiences of a company outsourcing engineering work. Was this work appropriate to BS, MS or Ph.D. level engineers? Was the company satisfied with the outcome?

5) Do you believe that outsourcing will affect your career? Why or why not?

6) Do you agree with Thomas Friedman's thesis that all foreign science and engineering students getting a Ph.D. at a US university should be given a green card? Find examples of foreign students who stayed in the US, and who became successful and famous entrepreneurs or innovators. How many engineering jobs did they create?

7) Find examples of foreign entrepreneurs who were educated in the US and returned to their native countries to found successful enterprises. Find biographical information on them that might indicate why they left the US.

Index

Made in the USA
Middletown, DE
09 June 2015